INTUITION

An Hachette UK Company
www.hachette.co.uk

First published in 2008 by Godsfield
Press, an imprint of Octopus Publishing
Group Ltd
Carmelite House
50 Victoria Embankment
London, EC4Y 0DZ
www.octopusbooks.co.uk

This edition is published in 2025.

This material was previously published
as *Working with Your Sixth Sense*

Distributed in the US by
Hachette Book Group
1290 Avenue of the Americas
4th and 5th Floors
New York, NY 10104

Distributed in Canada by
Canadian Manda Group
664 Annette St.
Toronto, Ontario, Canada M6S 2C8

ISBN 978-1-8418-1612-8

A CIP catalogue record for this book is
available from the British Library

Printed and bound in China

10 9 8 7 6 5 4 3 2 1

Publisher: Lucy Pessell
Designer: Isobel Platt
Editor: Feyi Oyesanya
Assistant Editor: Samina Rahman
Production Controller:
Sumayyah Waheed

Cover illustration:
Iryna Shkrabaliuk/iStock

Picture Credits:
iStock: Artur Charkin, Oleg Lyfar,
martinwimmer, naqiewei, Normform,
osherro, RLT_Images, Iryna
Shkrabaliuk, Svetlana Vdovina, tmn-art.

MIX
Paper | Supporting
responsible forestry
FSC
www.fsc.org   FSC® C016973

Acknowledgments: My sincere thanks
to Sandra Rigby for her insight, help
and support and to Lisa John for her
inspirational suggestions. Thanks also
to everyone at Godsfield who made
this book possible. Finally, special
thanks to Roy, Robert and Ruth for
their support, love and empathy as
I worked on this project.

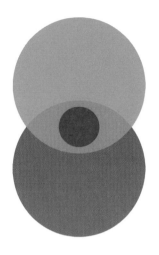

INTUITION

How to Discover Your Sixth Sense

THERESA CHEUNG

GODSFIELD

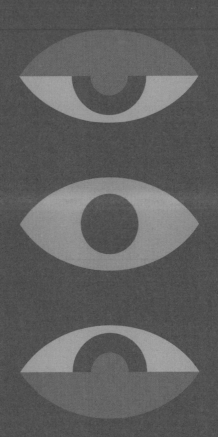

CONTENTS

Mysterious Butterflies

Many moons ago when this book was first born, the inception was (and is) my unshakable belief in sixth sense. A belief informed by my upbringing in a family of psychics; illustrated by my own intuitive experiences, writing and research and inspired by the countless true stories sent to me by my readers about their waking hunches and dreams coming true.

I remain confident that the insight and intuition igniting tools you will find here are as empowering and as relevant today as they have ever been. Perhaps even more so as what my younger self intuitively shared on first publication has now been fully illuminated by science.

In recent years I have collaborated with scientists, neuroscientists and psychologists researching intuition. I have learned that intuition research is booming and there is a growing consensus among scientists that it is an invisible super power within everyone. Our bodies really can sense the future – the scientific term is presentiment. And our brains really can sense the future before it happens, both when our eyes are wide open and wide shut when we are dreaming.

The infinite neuronal firings in your brain that enable you to think and dream were once described by the founder of modern neuroscience, Santiago Ramón y Cajal, (1852–1934) as 'mysterious butterflies of the soul.' And although mystery still surrounds the workings of the brain, cognitive scientists are increasingly drawn to the idea that the 'mysterious butterflies' that create your perception of your waking and dreaming world are inherently *predictive*. They help you sense what is yet to come and intuitively know what is in your best interests.

And, most important of all, this visionary research is proving that the single most important factor when it comes to unlocking your intuition is your belief in it. In many ways, being highly intuitive is *believing* in yourself. I sincerely hope this timely reissue will play its part in empowering your intuition and, in the process, help you believe that there is tremendous untapped power, wisdom and creativity within you.

Einstein once said that the greatest thing you can experience is the mysterious. Wise words indeed. But after reading this book and practising all the techniques, you will discover for yourself that mystery isn't something you experience. Mystery defines you. It is the real you.

The next time you see a butterfly, or view an image of one, or read or hear the word spoken, take this sign as the beautiful synchronicity it is. A loving reminder that mystery is not to be feared and you are – always have been and always will be – a deeply intuitive soul.

Note: Some of the exercises in this book do ask you to visualize, but if you struggle to form mental images, as a lot of us do (myself included) simply write down or describe to yourself – out loud or with your thoughts – what you want to visualize. It has the same transcendent effect. And inability to form mental images by day does not impact your night vision, AKA, your ability to 'see' images in your nocturnal dreams.

Theresa Cheung, 2024

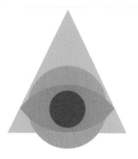

INTRODUCTION:
YOUR SILENT POWER

We are all born with a sixth sense, but most of us aren't aware of it, or use it only occasionally. A sixth sense is not something that some people possess and others lack; some people are simply more aware of their abilities or more naturally sensitive than others. Rest assured, however, that the potential is there within you; it is simply a forgotten art that needs to be rediscovered and developed.

Clues to your sixth sense

- Have you ever had dreams that later seemed to come true?
- Have there been times in your life when you experienced déjà vu, or the feeling that you have been through something before?
- Have you experienced an inexplicable attraction to someone?
- Have you ever had a hunch that something would happen and then it did?
- Do you sometimes just know what someone else is thinking?
- Have you ever stared at someone, thinking they can't see you, only to find that they suddenly turn round and stare right back at you?
- Have you ever thought of someone and then found they telephoned a few minutes later?
- Do you sometimes sense the atmosphere in a room or know when others are upset, angry or excited before they speak to you?
- Have you ever had a sudden feeling that you should, or should not, do something or be somewhere – then found out later that you should have listened to that feeling?

Even if you only answered 'maybe' to just one of these questions, it is an indication that you have had what appears to be the simplest, most basic kind of psychic (sixth-sense) experience.

How to use this book

In this book you can build on that basic level and learn how to do things you never dreamed to be possible. Just as you can become more aware of your other senses – those of sight, hearing, touch, taste and smell – so in the chapters that follow you will be shown how you can daily improve, develop and work with your sixth sense for your personal development, spiritual growth, self-healing and success.

Consider this book your first step into a world of endless potential. By means of the techniques you will learn here – relaxation, dream analysis, meditation, clairaudience, clairvoyance, clairsentience, remote viewing, mandala work, intuitive consciousness-raising, psychometry, telekinesis, telepathy, aura reading, scrying and many others – you will strengthen your sixth sense, finding natural ways to tap into your wellspring of intuitive wisdom.

As you read the book you will be given practical and safe guidance on every aspect of your psychic development and how you can experience it in everyday life. You will be taken stage by stage through those hunches and vague thoughts that, when put together, make up your psychic potential – your silent power. Develop that silent potential. Its power to enrich all aspects of your life will amaze you.

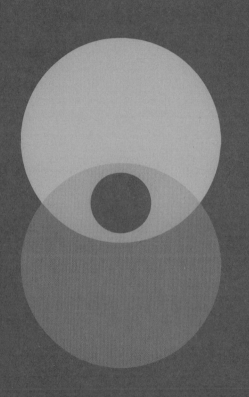

WHAT IS YOUR
SIXTH SENSE?

If you have ever had a feeling that something might happen and it did, or had a dream that came true, or thought something at exactly the same time someone else did, then you may be using your sixth sense without even realizing it.

Your sixth sense can help you in all aspects of your life – your relationships, your career, your family – but most of all it can help you realize your full potential and become the happy and successful person you are destined to be.

The exercises in this chapter are designed to help you become more aware of this world inside your head and beyond your senses – the world of your sixth sense, intuition or psychic power. Understanding the way you receive information from your sixth sense is a step towards building it, so in the pages that follow we look at three main areas of psychic ability: clairvoyance, clairaudience and clairsentience. As you read the descriptions and work through the exercises, see if any of your instincts draw you to any of these areas in particular.

CONNECTING TO YOUR
SIXTH SENSE

When most people think of a sixth sense, they tend to think of an intuitive power. After consideration, it becomes apparent that what we call 'intuition' is – as well as being a mental facility – also a super-sense, the cumulative power of all the senses: sight, hearing, taste, touch and smell. As we all possess intuition, we are therefore all able to unify our senses, giving us the power to find meaning in our lives, realize our potential and achieve personal fulfillment. In this book the terms intuition, sixth sense and psychic power are interchangeable.

Obviously we can't all be multi-millionaires or famous film stars, but by using our sixth sense we can find out what our true potential is and maximize it. In fact, like a telephone caller put on hold with crucial information to offer, your sixth sense already knows the answers to your problems – you just need to learn how to pay attention to it, interpret what it is trying to tell you and then do something about it.

Use it or lose it

All of us have a sixth sense. So, you may ask, why aren't more of us using it? Let's try to explain by giving an example. If someone lived in the dark for years, their eyes would adjust to the absence of light; over time that person would actually be able to see better in the dark than in the light. It's the same with your sixth sense. Once civilization and technology came along, people didn't have to rely as much on being super-alert to stay alive and keep away from danger, and they simply got lazy and stopped sensing things around them.

In other words, if you don't use your psychic ability, you lose it. Forget what you have seen on television or at the movies; psychic ability isn't going to appear magically without any effort on your part. You need to rediscover, train and develop it every day, in much the same way that you would build up your physical fitness. A fundamental principle of sixth sense – and, indeed, of this book – is that personal responsibility makes you the one accountable for discovering and developing your sixth sense, and for where you take your life from here.

Developing your sixth sense is a journey of rediscovery and self-discovery: rediscovering your inborn psychic ability and discovering who you are and where you are going. Once you understand this, you can begin to move forward, using what you discover to make the most of your life in every way. So where you do you start? You start by crossing a very special line – the line between your non-psychic side (your physical self) and your psychic side (your thoughts).

Symbols of all kinds surround us; the messages they bring can help you cross between the physical and psychic worlds.

AWAKENING TO
YOUR PSYCHIC ABILITY

Awakening to your psychic ability, or crossing the line between your non-psychic and psychic sides, isn't something you can do with your body. You have to do it with your mind. Having said that, you can't develop your sixth sense without physical awareness.

The non-psychic side of your life is dominated by your five senses. In this familiar world you rely entirely on your senses for finding things out. Eyes, nose, mouth, ears and skin all give you news about what is happening to you. Stop right now and look around. Really listen to the sounds, look at the sights, smell the air. The manifold richness of life is all around you, continually flooding in through your body's senses. Many of us take our senses for granted, but it is only when we become more aware of them that we can start to tell when we are getting information without using our physical senses.

The world beyond the senses

So what is on the other side, the psychic side? The answer is simple: your thoughts. Feeling, hearing and seeing your thoughts are the beginning of psychic development. Try looking at it like this: thoughts come from the world of the senses, but they can carry you over to the world beyond your senses. For example, you can imagine being at work or at home without actually being there, just as you can imagine someone you love without the need for their immediate physical presence. This is because you can feel and listen to your thoughts, and your thoughts can transcend time and place. Your thoughts may be all about the material world or what is happening outside you, but they take place inside you. Simply recognizing this distinction is the beginning of psychic awareness – an awareness of a world inside your head that is quite different from the physical world in which you live and work. This is the world where your psychic power will start to reveal itself. From now on you are going to develop a whole new way of seeing things.

The key to developing your sixth sense is your imagination. It is your imagination that can take you on your psychic adventures.

Identifying the real you

We have all had times in our lives when we suddenly see something that nobody else sees, hear something that no one else hears or simply know something out of the blue – a thought that arrives without prompting. These are times when you have learned or discovered something without using your five senses. Gradually, a whole new world is opening up to you. You can call it many things: psychic power, intuition, inner knowing, gut feeling or sixth sense. Better still, you could call it 'me'.

As you work through the exercises and techniques that follow, the world inside your head and beyond your senses should start to become a much more real place to you.

WATCHING YOURSELF

It might help to start by acting as an observer of your own life. Step outside yourself and take a look at what you think, feel, say and do. Don't criticize or judge; simply observe. This may sound a bit crazy, but it is a well-known technique for improving self-awareness. Watching yourself can really help you separate what you think and feel from who you are. You will see that throughout the day your thoughts and feelings constantly flow through you; and that, powerful though these thoughts and feelings are, they are really separate from you. You are the one who allows yourself to experience them. You are the one in charge.

The more you can separate what you think and feel from who you are, the more in charge of your life you will feel.

INTUITION

Intuition is knowing something, without being aware of how you know it. It is knowledge that seems to come to you from nowhere, a sudden awareness or insight without logical support. Although the origin of this knowledge cannot be deduced though step-by-step analysis, it is certainly real knowledge – be it the vagueness of a hunch, a gut instinct, vibe or feeling, or a vivid lightning bolt of understanding.

As we have seen, the terms intuition, sixth sense and psychic power are interchangeable in this book, because they all refer to the same truth: that each of us has a part of our consciousness that acts as a bridge between the physical and non-physical dimensions of our awareness or, as some like to describe it, our inner wisdom or higher mind. Simply put, we all have a part of ourselves that is better able to see the bigger picture of our lives, and our intuition, sixth sense or psychic ability can help us cross that bridge and enable us to listen to our inner wisdom. Acting with the guidance of our inner wisdom can put everything in perspective, leading us in the direction of our greatest happiness and fulfillment. Think about it! Isn't it true that some of the best decisions you have ever made began as impulses or ideas that came out of the blue, but just felt right?

What helps most with psychic growth are feelings of reverence and natural awe.

A psychic change of gear

Just as the food you eat nourishes your body, so your feelings (your intuition or hunches) are food for your inner world. As with nutrition, some psychic foods are better for you than others. A diet of self-interest, competitiveness, frustration and boredom will not produce a strong psychic sense, but there is one 'feeling' food that you will need more than anything else in developing your psychic sense. What is it? Respect. Believe it or not, respect for life, nature and the amazing world in which we live – combined with wonder and honest intention – is the richest food with which to stimulate your psychic growth.

By holding the idea of respect in your head as you work through the exercises that follow, you will give yourself a psychic change of gear, and your understanding will grow enormously. If you are having trouble grasping this, think back to when you were a child. Was there someone who inspired awe in you? If that doesn't help, think of spectacular things in the natural world – a waterfall, a rainbow, a sunset – that inspire awe. By tapping into your feelings of awe, wonder and respect, you will step up a gear in your psychic development.

If you can find and somehow rekindle veneration again, a rich cycle of psychic growth can occur.

PSYCHIC WORKOUTS

The following exercises are designed to help you become more aware of the world inside your head and beyond your senses. The exercises in this book are not tests and there are no right or wrong answers. Just try them and see how you feel. It may take time for you to catch on, so maintain a positive attitude. If possible, work with them every day and at different times. Think of them as psychic workouts that flex your sixth-sense muscles. And, as with any physical workout, you will benefit from a cool-down afterwards: any simple act that brings you back to normal, such as grabbing a snack, going for a walk, chatting to a friend or surfing the Internet.

Growth and decay

1. You can start to develop your psychic awareness by paying attention to things in nature that are in the process of growing and flourishing, and decaying and withering away. By doing this, you are starting to focus on the universal lifecycle. The more you do this, the more likely it is that you will start to feel as if you are a part of an energy force passing through and around you.

2. Focus your attention on a natural object: flowers growing in a pot, a playful puppy, the sun rising or setting, or leaves falling from the trees.

3. Once you have got used to the feelings and shapes of growth and decay, try to tune into them even when you don't have an object in front of you to inspire that vision. This is a completely new way of looking at things, so give yourself plenty of time. The idea is that growth and decay aren't just words or objects to you; they are living forces that evoke images or associations in your mind. This is the start of psychic vision.

4. You are now ready to move on to other themes, such as the world of colour; what feelings or images do certain colours inspire in you? Or you could contrast the feelings inspired in you by living things, such as animals or plants, with those provoked by inanimate things such as rocks or crystals.

Different levels

————

This is a simple thinking exercise that you can do at any time, anywhere. Choose something familiar that you see every day – your coat, for example. Now you are going to think about it on four different levels.

1. Just think about the coat itself. What colour is it? Where did you buy it? What good or bad times have you had wearing it?

2. Think of coats in general – everywhere.

3. Think of the purpose of coats: why do people wear them?

4. Think about coats in the abstract sense. For instance, they can be a symbol of protection and warmth, so let your mind linger on images of fire or comforting soup.

Staring at a plant

For this exercise, which is again designed to awaken your psychic vision, you need to stare at a plant. This isn't as odd as it sounds; in fact, it may be the hardest exercise in the book so far, so don't become discouraged if you don't get immediate results.

1. Observe a young plant closely, paying special attention to its colour, shape and texture. Let the following thought fill your mind: This plant will one day become a bigger plant.

2. Now picture in your mind this bigger plant – see what it will one day become.

3. In time you may begin to see a mist or cloud surrounding the plant, or an image in your mind of the plant in flower. It isn't the staring that produces this effect; it is your understanding that every living being is surrounded by energy and has a destiny in store for it. If you can't see anything yet, don't worry. Just thinking about this idea will help enormously with your psychic development.

Crystal ball reading does not depend on any special properties of the crystal; what produces results is your sincerity and state of mind.

TUNING IN

What do you think so far? Have the exercises helped open your mind? Now that you are becoming more open to the world of thoughts, which is your bridge between the non-psychic and psychic worlds, it is time to learn more about how you can receive psychic information. There are many ways in which such information can come to you, and each and every person has a specific way that works best for them.

METHODS OF
PSYCHIC AWARENESS

You can receive messages from your intuition or sixth sense through:

- CLAIRVOYANCE: mentally seeing what is happening in an unseen or out-of-sight dimension.
- CLAIRAUDIENCE: hearing what is beyond the normal audible range.
- CLAIRSENTIENCE: smelling or sensing what is unseen.
- PSYCHOMETRY: seeing without your eyes – tuning into objects, reading a person's character and even being able to tell their past and future.
- TELEPATHY: tuning into the thoughts of others and projecting your thoughts into another person's mind.
- DREAMING: tuning into psychic frequencies while asleep and bringing information back into everyday life by interpreting the symbols and images within the dream.
- DIVINATION: seeing into the future using psychic tools such as crystal balls, Tarot cards and tea leaves.
- PRECOGNITION: the knowledge of events before they take place.
- SPIRIT COMMUNICATION: the ability to communicate with spirits, also called channelling or mediumship.

Keep observing yourself

Understanding the way you receive information from your sixth sense is another step towards building it, and in the pages that follow you will be encouraged to discover the way you are most likely to receive psychic information. Don't worry if it isn't immediately clear to you which method of psychic awareness you are drawn to, or if you are drawn to more than one. For now, just keep observing yourself and thinking about the way you think. In time, things will fall naturally into place.

Don't try to force things, just keep the ideas of the last few pages firmly in the back of your mind. The more you feel sympathy in yourself with the ideas of respect and awe, the more your sixth sense will grow automatically without your worrying about it. The more you will realise that the most reliable place to look for guidance is your higher self.

CLAIRVOYANCE

Have you ever seen images in your head? Perhaps you saw yourself passing an exam before you heard that you had passed? Perhaps you visualized yellow flowers in your mind's eye and, when you went on a date, saw that each table at the restaurant had a vase with little yellow flowers? If you have had experiences similar to these, you might be receiving psychic information through clairvoyance.

Clairvoyance comes from a French word meaning 'clear seeing'. It is the power to see an event or an image in the past, present or future. This type of sight is not achieved with your physical eyes, but with your inner eyes. A person with clairvoyant ability can receive information in the form of visual images or symbols. For some clairvoyants, it is almost like having a movie screen inside their head with images scrolling across it. Other clairvoyants may see symbols that they learn to interpret, or people and animals in spirit form.

Do you process information visually?

If you have strong visual skills, you may be particularly attuned to developing clairvoyance. If you answer 'yes' to any of the questions below, you may be a strongly visual person and therefore more likely to receive information through clairvoyance.

- Do you think in pictures?
- Do you notice what things look like, rather than how they sound, feel, taste or smell?
- Are you an art lover?
- Are you fascinated by the appearance of people, objects or the environment?

Subjective clairvoyance

Many clairvoyants get their insights internally – through their mind's eye; this is called subjective clairvoyance. It can come in the form of lights, images, symbols, colours or dreams, but some clairvoyants describe the images they receive as being projected from their 'third eye' – as if it were a television or movie screen just in front of their forehead. This third eye or inner eye, which is one of the seven main chakras (see page 165), gives them the ability to see or sense something without using their physical eyesight.

*The Ajna yantra, or forehead chakra, indicates the position
of the third eye, just above the eyebrows.
The Downward-Facing Dog (Adho Mukha Svanasana)
pose helps to activate the third-eye chakra.*

Although some of us may have greater natural abilities that relate to other psychic senses, we all have the ability to develop subjective clairvoyance. The secret to unlocking this ability lies in your imagination. To develop your clairvoyant ability you need to allow yourself to dream, visualize and fantasize. The trick is to get there before your rational mind can sort, assess and figure out what to do.

Many of the exercises in the next chapter (see pages 53–63) will help you develop your ability to think in pictures, and thus your clairvoyant potential to see the future in pictures. For now you might want to try the following exercise.

Colour vision

This exercise is all about impressions, so try not to think too much about what you are doing.

1. Cut out a 13 cm (5 in) square piece of white paper.

2. Using a felt tip, draw a circle and colour it blue. Now colour around that circle in orange.

3. Look at this card for two minutes. Don't stare too intently; just keep your eyes focused on the card for as long as you can.

4. Now close your eyes. You will see a faint likeness of the card in your inner vision, although the colours might change. Watch this inner image until it fades. Make no attempt to alter it.

5. Try to do this every day for five days. After a while you should find that you see the card clearly in your mind whenever you wish. All you need to do is close your eyes and wait!

6. Keep doing this for another week. Then one day, when you see the card with your eyes closed, simply open your eyes. The image should not disappear, but will be hanging there suspended in space – a vision.

Objective clairvoyance

Have you ever caught a glimpse of someone out of the corner of your eye, only to discover that they aren't there? Have you ever seen someone who has died, or who is somewhere else? If you have, you might be one of those extremely rare individuals who is an objective clairvoyant. Such a clairvoyant can see people, animals and objects in spirit form as if they were physically present.

Visions of this nature can be linked to messages of encouragement and wisdom, and their purpose is always safe and good.

Probably the best known objective clairvoyant is Nostradamus (1503–66). He is said to have gazed into a bowl of water to receive his famous visions of the future.

CLAIRAUDIENCE

Have you ever heard sounds or voices that you know are real, even though you know they aren't happening in the 'real world'? For example, a bell ringing, a baby crying or a song that keeps repeating itself? Have you ever been convinced that you heard someone calling you, even when they weren't? Have you ever heard voices warning you not to do something, or telling you to do something? If you have had these or similar experiences, you may be receiving psychic impressions through clairaudience. Clairaudience literally means 'clear hearing' and is the ability to receive psychic impressions through sound.

Do you process information aurally?

If you answer 'yes' to any of the following questions, the chances are that you have a tendency towards clairaudience.

- Are you a good listener?
- Do you describe your experiences in terms of the sounds you hear or what you are listening to?
- Do you find certain sounds and noises unbearable?
- Do you have a flair for words?
- When you meet someone or go to a particular place, does a familiar song or piece of music pop into your head?

Listen to your inner ear

Clairaudient words of wisdom may seem like bits of common sense from a familiar inner voice – and indeed that is what they are. We all receive a constant stream of information from our intuition, and a certain amount is clairaudient. You just need to remember to listen.

1. Seat yourself in a quiet place, close your eyes and relax. Put your concentration on the right, lower side of your head, to a point in the region of your inner ear. Now simply wait.

2. Through practice you will be able to tell if the voices you hear come from your intuition or are merely your own daily thoughts. Listen carefully: your intuition speaks to you in a kind, loving and gentle way; self-talk tends to be a little harsher and more critical.

3. You may find that you have a particular psychic ear – meaning that either your left or right ear is the one in which you will hear psychic impressions.

Holding a shell to your ear can help to bring you closer to the voices of the sea.

Use your psychic hearing

You may not realize it, but your ears convey feelings to you.

1. Think about your favourite song. Does it make you feel a certain way?

2. Now apply this to the world around you. Listen to what you can hear right now, distinguishing between sounds produced by lifeless things, such as a bell ringing or a door slamming, and sounds that come from humans or animals. What feeling does an inanimate sound inspire in you? What feeling does a sound from a living thing engender in you?

3. The sound from living things is the key to psychic insight. Notice what the living sound tells you, then try to bridge that gap and unite yourself with that feeling. It doesn't matter whether or not you like the sound – just try to connect with it. Fill yourself inwardly with the feeling of that sound.

Hearing through sound

Your new ability to be sensitive to sound can spread throughout your life. You are starting to 'hear' with your emotions and your thoughts, rather than with your ears. Natural sounds can affect you deeply. Things begin to speak to you, not through words, but through noise and sound.

CLAIRSENTIENCE

Clairsentience is often described as clear thinking or clear knowing. It is the most common way in which people receive psychic information, especially women and children, who tend to be more emotionally based than men. Clairsentience is the ability to receive intuitive insight or information through your senses of smell, touch and taste. Whether you know it or not, you have probably already received information in this way. For example, you may have met someone and felt apprehensive or excited for no apparent reason; you may have sensed an atmosphere when you entered a room. These experiences are common psychic abilities but are not well recognized.

Do you process information emotionally?

If you answer 'yes' to any of the questions below, you probably have strong clairsentient tendencies.

- Are you empathetic or compassionate towards others?
- Are you often affected by the moods of people close to you, such as partners, friends, family members and colleagues?
- Do you get a bad taste in your mouth, butterflies in your stomach or a tight feeling in your chest when something doesn't feel right?
- Do you smell things for no reason, such as roses when you are feeling happy?
- Can you sense the atmosphere in a room before anyone has spoken to you?

Developing your potential

In the next two chapters you will find various exercises to help develop your clairsentient potential. These are the starting points for most people, but if you are not sure how your psychic ability manifests itself, try the exercise below.

Tuning into a day at the beach

This exercise can help you get in touch with the way you receive psychic information.

1. Close your eyes and breathe deeply. Gently relax. In your mind's eye, imagine yourself on a sandy beach on a beautiful sunny day. You can smell the sea air; you can hear the seagulls. A warm, gentle breeze lifts your hair. You hear and see the waves gently lapping on the shore. You can feel the heat of the sun on your skin. Your feet are bare and you feel the sand between your toes. You bend down to touch the cool water. You walk along the beach, feeling calm, relaxed and happy. You see an ice-cream stand ahead and buy an ice-cold vanilla cone. You taste it in your mouth and feel the refreshing coolness slide down your throat.

2. Now open your eyes slowly and think about what you experienced. Which one of your senses was it easiest for you to get in touch with? Was it sight or visual images (clairvoyance)? Was it sound (clairaudience)? Or was it smell, touch and taste (clairsentience)?

The way ahead

To help you get as full a picture as possible of yourself and your talents, this chapter has introduced you to the three main areas of psychic ability: clairvoyance, clairaudience and clairsentience. Many of the exercises in this book are designed to develop one or more of these areas. You may find that you are drawn to all three methods, but as you read on you may also begin to notice that your instincts attract you to one method in particular. Do you already have abilities in this area, or do you have a hunch that you might be able to develop them?

WORKING
WITH YOUR
SUBCONSCIOUS

Although the media typically presents us with images of sorrow and suffering, every day wonderful things are also happening to men and women from all walks of life. People fall in love, go on holiday, get the job they want, gain an unexpected windfall, pass exams, achieve their goals, laugh and have fun.

Wonderful things can happen to you too, when you start using the magic power of your subconscious mind.

Intuitive flashes originate in your subconscious mind, and in this chapter we explore how to tap into your subconscious powers to maximize your chances of success and happiness in all aspects of your life. You will learn about the awesome power of your imagination and how techniques such as visualization, relaxation, concentration, meditation and working with mandalas and mantras can add a whole new dimension of creativity, excitement and happiness to your psychic development and to your life as a whole.

THE LEVELS OF CONSCIOUSNESS

It is easier to notice, listen to and train your intuitive powers if you have an understanding of the place from which those intuitive flashes originate: your subconscious mind. There are three levels of consciousness that play a role in psychic development: the conscious, the subconscious and the superconscious. All three must balance the messages they receive from each other.

Your conscious mind is in charge of reasoning, analysing and making critical decisions. In order for it to be efficient it needs to maintain objectivity. However, this isn't always easy because it constantly receives information from the subconscious and superconscious minds.

Your subconscious mind is like a giant computer, taking in thousands of bits of information every day – information that slips past your conscious attention, yet is nevertheless stored away. Every detail of every experience you have had since the beginning of your life is gathered here. It would be overwhelming for your conscious mind to process every detail of every event, so the mind files all this detail away into its huge storage library. If, however, the subconscious is jogged – by necessity, or by various psychic-development techniques, such as visualization, meditation or relaxation – it can release helpful information back to the conscious mind.

The subconscious mind is therefore far more powerful, and knows a great deal more, than the conscious mind, because it has the ability to retain and recall memories when they are needed. More significantly, the subconscious mind is also part of an infinite power that can be called the superconscious or universal mind. This is the place where spontaneous insights, hunches, gut instincts, inner wisdom or sixth sense comes from. If you do not tap into the treasure trove of insight stored in your subconscious mind, you are denying yourself the greatest chance of happiness, success and fulfilment.

Tapping into the subconscious

If you want to tap into your subconscious or creative powers, you need first to build your imagination. Imagination builds cities. The subconscious mind doesn't know the difference between reality and fantasy or imagination. Ideas that are formed in your mind are real, and everything that you tell the subconscious mind to be the truth is the truth. Second, you need to learn to control your thoughts. Psychics and mystics believe that through thought-control techniques, such as relaxation, concentration and meditation, you can tap into your subconscious mind and thereby influence the events that occur in your life. When you meditate, you set up powerful forces that emanate from yourself and influence the world around you.

Your subconscious mind is a storehouse of information.

MAKING YOUR SACRED SPACE

In the pages that follow you will learn how to build your imagination and your powers of concentration. But before you do that, you have to do some searching first – for a special place in which you can do your psychic work.

Your sacred space is the actual place in the physical world where you carry out your psychic-development work. Sacred spaces come in all shapes and sizes; there is no right way to create one – just make sure that you feel comfortable there. Your space doesn't need to be large: it can be the corner of a room, or simply a portable box with a candle and a special cloth that you carry around with you. Sacred spaces can be located anywhere, but it is up to you to make yours special to you. You are the one who needs to make a bridge between worlds in order to create new possibilities for yourself. Making a sacred space sets up a place where you can tap into your sixth sense.

A doorway to another dimension

Having a time and place where you will not be interrupted (whether by phones, other forms of intrusion or by other people) is the most important part of your sacred space. Remember that this is a special time for you: this place represents your sanctuary and your doorway to another dimension. Creating your sacred space changes the atmosphere around you to one that is softer, calmer and more peaceful. This is a shift from the outer to the inner world, and throughout this book you will be learning how to awaken your psychic powers in this sacred space.

DO'S AND DON'TS OF
YOUR SACRED SPACE

- In a perfect world the guidelines given below would be easy to follow. In the real world they are sometimes hard to accomplish. Just do the best you can – they are only guidelines; they are not essential, and some people may find they don't need a quiet spot or haven, for they can practise their psychic skills at any time, anywhere.

DO:

- Find a place where you won't be interrupted or disturbed.
- Choose objects that are special to you.
- Use soft lights or candles.
- Surround yourself with comforting sounds – gentle music, sounds from nature or even just silence.

DON'T:

- Clutter your space with unnecessary objects; less really is more.
- Use bright lights – they can be distracting when you try to relax.
- Bring your mobile phone; turn it off when you enter your sacred space.

Sacred spaces come in all shapes and sizes. There is no right way to create one – just make sure that you are comfortable.

RELAXATION AND GROUNDING

Wherever and however you decide to work, there are two things that are important for your psychic development: relaxation and grounding.

Relaxation is vital for working with your sixth sense, because the pressures of daily life can keep you from receiving and understanding messages from your subconscious mind. There are two good kinds of relaxation technique to learn – progressive relaxation and rhythmic breathing – and before you start any psychic exercise, you may want to begin with one of these two techniques.

Progressive relaxation

This is a wonderful way to begin your psychic work, because the more relaxed you are, the easier it is to get in touch with your psychic power.

1. Lie on the floor and make yourself comfortable. Take a deep breath and tense all your muscles.

2. As you breathe out, release the tension and send warm, soothing thoughts and energy to every part of your body, starting with your feet and moving up to the top of your head. You can do this by saying to yourself, 'My feet are relaxed . . . my ankles are relaxed . . . my knees are relaxed', and onwards to the top of your head.

Rhythmic breathing

You can use this method to relax at any time – before psychic work, prior to a job interview, after a long day or even if you can't get to sleep at night.

1. Begin rhythmic breathing from your stomach, breathing naturally, but slowly.

2. Slowly inhale through your nostrils for a count of five.

3. Hold for a count of five, and then exhale slowly for a count of five.

4. Imagine and feel warm energy flowing through your body. Feel the pause of peacefulness in between each breath.

Grounding

Every time you finish your psychic exercises you need to ground yourself and reconnect with the physical world, so that you can return to your daily life. Grounding can be different for everyone, so here are some examples of how you might do it:

- Try some stretches to reinvigorate yourself.
- Make a cup of tea.
- Eat a snack.
- Call a friend.
- Go for a walk or do some stretching.
- Write down your psychic experiences in a journal.

THE POWER OF IMAGINATION

In order to connect with your subconscious mind and to strengthen your sixth sense, you have to trust your imagination. Imagination is the foundation for psychic development; it is your imagination that will take you on your first psychic adventure.

Most of us neglect or dismiss our imagination, but it is really the key to everything you do. To develop psychically, you need to allow yourself to dream, fantasize and play. The trick is to get there before your conscious mind can sort, assess and figure out what to do. Of course, being rational is important, but when you're developing your sixth sense, it's all about your imagination.

Imagination plays a key part in everything we do.
It is a powerful human sense and needs training.

Picture this

Can you think of a time when a flash of imagination inspired you to try something new? Perhaps you looked at your living room and – in a flash – saw it in a different way. With a bit of paint, you created a whole new room.

Strengthening your imagination is the way towards psychic insight. To understand your imagination, however, you need to think in images. Words are not the language of your imagination. The exercises that follow will help you develop creative ways to use your imagination and strengthen your psychic powers. From now on, every time you do an exercise, try to set the mood by working in your sacred space (see pages 46–7) if you can, and by doing some relaxation exercises (see pages 48–9) before you work. And don't forget to ground yourself (see page 50) when you have finished.

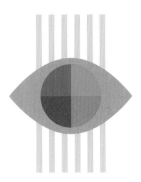

Be swept away

This exercise will help to stimulate your imagination from the outside.

1. Find an illustrated book of fairy tales and spend some time just looking at the pictures. Think back to when you were a child and your parents read you a fairy tale. While you may remember hearing the story, what you probably remember most are the pictures and the feelings they provoked. Whether it was the sun setting, a fire-breathing dragon, the princess's long hair or a knight's horse, the picture was real to you and you were absorbed by it. For a few moments you experienced it deeply in your imagination.

2. As you look at the pictures now with adult eyes, you may begin to notice feelings inside yourself that feel both familiar and new at the same time. This is a sign that the pictures are working their magic and that you are getting through to your psychic centre via your imagination.

From I to Y

This exercise will help to stimulate your imagination from the inside.

1. Draw a large I and a large Y close to each other on a piece of paper. Look at both letters, then cover up the Y shape with your hand and look only at the I. In your mind's eye, let the I transform itself into a Y. See the line dividing and turning outwards.

2. Try it again, only this time try to see one arm growing faster than the other.

3. Do it again and see one arm waiting for the other to complete before it moves. See in your mind's eye one of the arms moving and, when it stops, the other arm moving.

CREATIVE VISUALIZATION

When you imagine or visualize something, you see mental images, and these images have a meaning. Visualization is important because psychic messages often come to us in the form of images. Your job is to find out what these images are trying to tell you.

The best way to work on visualization skills is to practise. Here are some exercises to help you do just that. Be sure to go to your sacred space (see pages 46–7) when you do these exercises, so that you won't be disturbed.

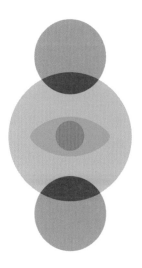

The cross

At first you may think you can't see anything, but keep trying and you will succeed. With a bit of practice and patience, anyone can visualize.

1. Close your eyes and imagine a cross – any kind of cross that you like.

2. Hold this image in your mind and slowly rotate it until it is upside down.

3. Continue to rotate it until it has gone a full 360 degrees and is upright again.

4. When you have finished, leave your cross upright. You should always leave your visualization as you find it; if you don't, you might feel a bit unbalanced afterwards.

Live your dreams

As you work increasingly with visualization, you may be able to visualize future events in your life. You might be able to keep your mind on what you want to such a degree that you can actually see the future happening here and now. Think of a forthcoming event that is important to you. Perhaps it is a job interview or a social engagement, and your goal is to create a good impression or do your best. Follow these steps:

1. Make sure you are somewhere quiet where you will not be disturbed and get comfortable.

2. Slow down your breathing and take some deep breaths to relax.

3. When you feel relaxed enough, take one really deep breath and – as you slowly draw it in – feel a tingling sensation run all the way down your body from the top of your head to the tips of your toes.

4. Spend a few moments just listening to the silent air around you, and let your imagination go where it will.

5. See and hear things in your future as if they were happening now – as if you have already achieved your chosen goal. See yourself being offered the dream job, doing well, creating a good impression or getting excellent results.

6. Intensify your vision by bringing the whole range of your senses into play: see what you are wearing, what things smell like and how things taste.

7. When you are ready, bring yourself back to reality by counting slowly up to ten.

Picture perfect

This is a really creative and fun visualization exercise that will boost your clairvoyant ability.

1. First of all, choose a picture that you like; it can be a photograph, a painting or a drawing. Try to pick something calm or uplifting rather than scary or troubling, and make sure your picture isn't crowded with too many things.

2. Find a place – preferably your sacred space – where no one else is around and you are not going to be disturbed. Take the picture with you.

3. Sit in a comfortable position with the picture on the floor or on a chair about 1 m (3 ft) away from you. Take several deep breaths to relax.

4. Now tune out everything else from your mind and look at your picture for a few minutes. Try to memorize every detail in it. What colours are used? What image from the picture jumps out at you?

5. When you're ready, close your eyes and try to remember everything in the picture. Describe it to yourself. Recall every detail, however small or insignificant. Try to see the picture in both words and images, visualizing it in your mind's eye. Perhaps the picture is even better in your head than it is in real life.

>>>

6. Open your eyes and take a second look at the picture. What did you remember? What did you forget? How many different colours were there? You will be surprised how quickly you forget things. If you have forgotten a lot, try going back to the beginning and doing the exercise again.

7. Now close your eyes and imagine that you are slowly melting into the picture. Stand in your picture, look at everything and see it all in your head. Take a walk in your picture. Don't be embarrassed to interact with the picture: no one is watching you, so be as open as you can. As you walk around your picture, try to start a conversation, if there are any people in the picture. Enjoy the mood of the picture – feel it in every part of your body.

8. When you feel ready, slowly walk out of the picture and back to reality. Take your time coming back to reality after this exercise, for it is quite a head trip.

9. Once you have returned, ground yourself (see page 50). These earthbound activities afterwards are just as important as the exercise itself.

EVERYDAY VISUALIZATION EXERCISES

You have already begun improving your imagination. Now it is time to take things to the next level. Here are some fast, fun ways to boost your visualization skills and your clairvoyant potential. Try to do them on a daily basis.

Visualize everyday objects

This exercise lays the foundation for psychic vision.

1. Practise closing your eyes and visualizing everyday objects, such as your watch, your keys, your mobile phone, and so on, in as much detail as possible.

People-peeping

Remember that imagination is a way of seeking, so use this exercise to hone your powers of imagination.

1. The next time you find yourself in a busy area where there are lots of people, such as a station, airport or shopping mall, find somewhere comfortable to sit and simply watch the passers-by going about their lives (don't stare, because this could alarm people).

2. Inevitably someone will catch your eye more than anyone else. As they walk by, keep their image in your mind and try to imagine where they are going or what their job is. Don't guess – try to visualize it. Pay attention to everything that you feel and imagine.

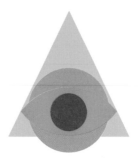

Ring-a-ling

This exercise will help you practise your ability to visualize someone who is not visually present and, by so doing, develop your clairvoyant potential.

1. The next time the phone rings, close your eyes and try to visualize who is calling before you answer. What first pops into your mind? If nothing comes to mind, ask yourself questions: Male? Female? Relative? Friend?

2. Partial answers do count. If you thought it was your sister calling, but it was your aunt, you still knew it was a woman, and that's a great start.

SO MANY WAYS TO VISUALIZE

There are endless ways to visualize. Here are some other suggestions that you can try at any time, anywhere:

- When you get a present or package, try to imagine what is inside. You can do the same with a letter – and before opening, try to imagine who sent it.
- When someone comes to the door, try to visualize who it is before answering.
- If the light on your answerphone is flashing, imagine whose messages are on it before you hit the 'play' button.
- In the morning before you head outdoors, try to imagine what the colour of the first car you see will be, what your colleagues at work will be wearing, and so on.
- Close your eyes and make a mental list of everything in your bedroom, and see in your mind's eye where these things are. Then create a picture of your room in your head.

CONCENTRATION

Concentration is the ability to focus on a chosen project and ignore what is irrelevant to it. First you must choose a project from the many others requiring your attention, then you must have the discipline to ignore all else.

Think of a time when you were so focused on what you were doing that you were able to block out all distractions. How can you re-create this level of concentration when doing your psychic exercises? If you don't think you can, try the exercise below and think again.

Walking backwards

This exercise will improve your concentration and boost your psychic ability. You don't have to walk backwards physically – you only have to remember things backwards.

1. The evening is the best time to perform this exercise, so before you go to bed choose a quiet, comfortable place where you can pay attention to your thoughts and won't be interrupted.

2. Take a deep breath to relax your body and prepare your mind.

3. Start from this moment and remember the events of your day backwards until you reach the moment you got up.

4. If you get stuck, go back a bit and then work forward to untangle yourself. Your mind will have a tendency to wander, but don't force things or feel tense; simply shift your focus back to the task in hand. You may only manage five- or ten-second bursts, but this is enough to help you become more open to your psychic impressions.

Concentration creation

This is such a powerful exercise to improve your concentration that you might want to practise it every day.

1. Make sure you aren't tired or hungry, then remove as many distractions as you can. Sit in a relaxed and upright position on the floor or in a chair that is comfortable, but not too comfortable.

2. Close your eyes and tell yourself firmly that you are 'good' at concentrating. By repeating 'I'm good at concentrating' you are programming your subconscious mind to believe that you have this skill. Repeat these words in whatever way suits you: write them, read them or say them over and over again.

3. Now give your mind a one-minute assignment. Tell it that you are going to write, read or say 'I'm good at concentrating' for one whole minute. Set an alarm and do the one-minute assignment with all your attention. The first few times you try this your mind may start to wander. Don't get upset – just be patient and persist. Remember: you are the one who controls what goes on in your mind. If you become aware you are thinking about something else, stop, say 'no' and return to your assignment with greater intensity.

4. When you are able to concentrate for one whole minute without being distracted, increase the period to two, three, four and then five minutes. Then make it harder for yourself. Introduce distractions: turn on the television, keep your eyes open, sit in a busy room. Repeat the exercise under these conditions until you are able to concentrate for five minutes.

5. This may take about three or four weeks to master, so don't worry if you don't get the hang of it right away. Once you are able to concentrate your mind, you can transfer these skills to your psychic development.

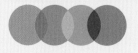

MEDITATION

The ultimate form of concentration is meditation. Meditation can recharge you, and reduce stress and anxiety. It can also help you receive intuitive guidance, because it relaxes your mind and makes you less easily distracted. Over time, a daily meditation of ten minutes will work wonders for your psychic development.

If you feel uncomfortable with the term 'meditation', try thinking of it as a time of stillness, quiet or even prayer. Try meditating at different times of the day to see which works best for you.

A golden doorway

The following exercise can help you connect with your intuition and psychic senses.

1. Relax, breathe deeply and imagine yourself standing in a doorway that glows with golden light. Visualize yourself surrounded by light energy. Tell yourself that you are safe, and that you will listen to your intuition.

2. Imagine that you can smell flowers and hear beautiful music. The place on the other side of the door is bright and inviting; you know that you are standing on the threshold of your unique psychic potential.

3. When you are ready, see yourself stepping through this doorway and finding yourself on the other side, bathed in a bright golden light and feeling warm and comfortable. The sounds and smells are even sweeter, you feel secure and stable, and the ground beneath your feet is firm. Stay here for a while and enjoy the feeling of the place; take note of any particular ideas or thoughts, but don't dwell on them.

4. When ready, gently stretch and open your eyes. Sit for a few moments before going back to your daily life.

Fly away

This simple exercise is a good starting point if you haven't meditated before. The more you meditate, the more naturally it will come to you; the greater control you will have over your thoughts; and in turn the more power you will have over your life.

1. Sit or lie down in your sacred space (see pages 46–7). Most people prefer to sit upright, but if you prefer lying down, that's fine. Make sure that your back is supported or straight, and that your body is open – don't cross your arms and legs; if you are physically open, you are more likely to be emotionally open.

2. Allow your eyes to close. Breathe in deeply, taking in a long, slow breath from your stomach, filling your lungs completely, gently holding the breath in for a moment and then releasing the air slowly. Focus on nothing but your breathing.

3. As you breathe, tell yourself that you are willing to develop your psychic potential. Let your fears, doubts and negative thoughts dissolve in a haze of golden light. If distracting thoughts enter your mind, imagine them turning into a beautiful bird or butterfly before flying away, leaving you calm, clear and still.

4. When you feel ready, slowly open your eyes, stretch and return to normal.

MANDALAS AND MANTRAS

Many people find that they can't focus when they try to meditate. If you're having a hard time concentrating, try one of these techniques. But however you choose to meditate, don't worry – there is no right or wrong way. It's a very personal thing, and whatever works for you is best.

Mandalas

Mandala is the Sanskrit word for 'circle'. It refers not to the shape of the circle itself, but to the circle of life. Mandalas are a beautiful aid to meditation: these wonderful (usually circular) designs draw your eye to their centre, which helps your mind to focus. When creating a mandala, the artist tries to coordinate the life circle with the universal circle, reflecting how each life fits into the larger whole, and how the inner and outer circles can unite. You can buy or order mandalas or, better still, design and make one yourself. Once you have found a mandala that inspires you, put it in front of you and gaze into its centre, letting your focus soften a little. Breathe slowly, deeply and rhythmically.

Using a mandala to meditate is one of the more visual ways to work with your sixth sense.

Mantras

If visual methods don't do it for you, try the sound-orientated approach – use a mantra during your meditation. A mantra (from the Sanskrit word meaning 'instrument of thought') is a sound, word or phrase that you repeat over and over again to keep your mind focused. The sound is intended to resonate in the body and evoke certain images during meditation. The Hebrew word shalom (peace) is commonly used as a mantra. Other frequently used words are om, 'love', 'peace' and 'joy'. Any word that is sacred to you, that evokes a special feeling or quality that you seek to develop, is a good one to try out. Simply close your eyes, breathe deeply and focus your attention on that one word, to the exclusion of all else.

Tracing labyrinths

The labyrinth is an ancient symbol of the spiritual journey to the centre. Walking through a labyrinth, or tracing its pattern with your fingers, can bring a deep sense of peace and harmony. Perhaps it is because you must focus on one step at a time, trusting that the journey will always lead to the centre, even when it appears that you are travelling in the opposite direction – heading the opposite way to where you think you need to be. By tracing the circuit of the labyrinth, you enable feelings, sensations, memories and images from your subconscious to rise to the surface, providing insights to solve problems and provoking a deep sense of calm and harmony.

Still can't concentrate?

Concentration so that you can tap into the power of your subconscious mind is crucial for psychic development; but if you are finding it impossible to concentrate, don't worry – you are not alone. Life is full of pressures and it is no wonder that some people find it hard to concentrate. That is why the chapters that follow are all about finding ways to further develop your psychic powers, helping you attain the focus that is crucial for success – not just in psychic development, but in the rest of your life, too.

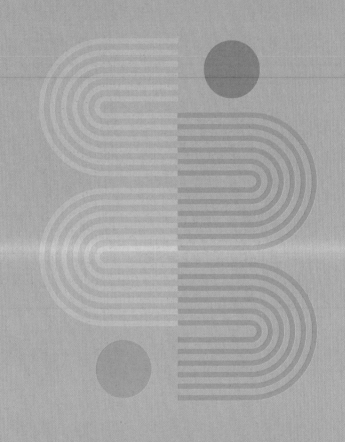

WORKING WITH PEOPLE

Telepathy may be one of the most common forms of intuitive experience that people have. For example, you may recall receiving a letter from someone you were thinking about, or you may have a bought a present for someone when they were just about to buy that item for themselves. Incidents like this may have occurred many times, but you may simply have dismissed them as guesswork or coincidence.

But if you have a knack for knowing what other people are thinking, you could be reading minds without realizing it.

In this chapter there are numerous exercises to develop your ability to read minds and understand people better. Even if you don't think you are particularly gifted in this area, it is worth working through them, as research has shown that empathy – the foundation stone for telepathy – is a universal human trait. You will also learn how to send and receive thoughts and how to read auras: the electromagnetic energies surrounding all living things, which contain our thoughts and feelings and which can be seen or sensed by psychics.

EMPATHY

As you have already learned, psychic power, or your sixth sense, is really another name for (or a natural extension of) an ability that we all have – intuition or gut instinct. Your intuition may tell you to call a friend and, when you do, you find out they really need to talk or are in some kind of trouble. Or you think of an old friend for no reason and then bump into them later that day.

Your gut instinct can also tell you a lot about people (whether you know them well or not), and the exercises that follow will help you develop your ability to read minds and communicate psychically with others. As you work through the exercises, remember that it is generally best to take a positive view of other people, because you are more likely to find positive qualities in others if you look for them, rather than anticipating the worst. Sometimes you just have a sense that it is safe to get close to someone, while at other times you may have nagging feelings of doubt. However irrational your gut feelings may seem, you should always try to understand and listen to them.

Every moment of awareness and empathy with others helps you appreciate all that you are.

Relating to other people

We all radiate a vast amount of information about ourselves, and every experience we have had in our lives leaves an impression on us. We also all have a level of natural clairsentient ability (see page 38) that helps us relate to those around us. One way to describe this ability would be to call it empathy. Empathy is feeling what someone else feels, or seeing things from another person's point of view. Psychics often use this natural empathy or understanding of others to help them guide and support people to make the most of their talents and abilities.

Have you ever imagined what it would be like to be someone else? Have you ever sensed feelings of joy, loss, sadness or excitement before someone who is actually experiencing them tells you about them? This is empathy at work, and it is possible to develop empathy so strongly that, just by touching someone, you can feel and experience what they feel and experience. Do be careful, though. Some people are more naturally empathetic than others, and you need to make sure that you don't become oversensitive and lose touch with what you are actually feeling. When you start to understand others better you develop the gift of empathy. If you choose to use this gift to give support and guidance to others, it shows a compassionate nature.

Working with others and being part of a team is a simple way to learn empathy and compassion.

HANDLING SENSITIVITY

Developing your sixth sense is one part of the story. Learning how to turn it on and off so that you don't become too sensitive is another. Psychic development will increase your potential for empathetic responses to people and places around you. For instance, you may no longer be able to ignore things the way you used to. You may see and feel things you don't want to.

When you are empathetic, someone else's feelings, emotions and attitudes can affect you so strongly that they almost feel like your own. An example might be that your brother breaks his leg and you feel pain in your own leg. When you develop your psychic ability, outside impressions tend to register more strongly, and you are more likely to receive impressions of feelings and situations that are not your own.

How sensitive are you?

If you answer 'yes' to any of the questions below, the chances are that you are a sensitive, empathetic person and need to protect yourself.

- Are you easily persuaded by others to do things you normally wouldn't do?
- Do your moods change as you go from one group to another?
- Do you feel drained after being with people?
- Do you need lots of time alone?
- Do you always seem to know what others are feeling?
- Are you a touchy-feely person?
- Do you have a tendency to take on other people's problems?

Listening to the problems of others does not mean they become your problems.

Cutting the thread

If you are naturally empathetic and find it hard to disconnect from others, try visualizing a way to separate yourself from them. You might imagine that you are cutting a thread between you and the other person, or you could visualize going into a special room and closing the door. You may even need to disconnect from loved ones in this way. You will reconnect again, but you need to have some time every day when you are not linked to others, so that you can feel more objective and calm.

It may help to visualize a protective bubble around you that no one can enter. Call upon the part of yourself that knows how to detach itself when feelings you get from others or your environment become overwhelming.

You can visualize a bubble around you to help turn your psychic gift on and off.

A PSYCHIC LOOK AT
THE HUMAN BODY

While we often look at the human body as a complex anatomical system, we will take a different approach here. By taking a psychic view of the body, you will learn to read and understand people better. There is a whole world of meaning in the human body that can touch and inspire your growing psychic perceptions and your intuitive understanding of yourself and others.

The head

Have you ever watched someone nodding off to sleep in a car or train? The head drops, then they wake and the head comes up again. It's a battle for the head to stay on top. The head likes to think of itself as king or queen of the castle – and it is. The next time you are with a group of people, be aware of their heads. Watch how their heads move. If you copy the way someone else's head moves, you may be able to generate within you a feeling for the emotions they might be experiencing.

The face

Face-reading can help you read and understand people better. The ancient art of physiognomy is 3,000 years old and it assigns each feature a meaning: the eyebrows show the amount of drive and our mental and creative energies; the nose relates to career and financial capacities; the mouth to emotional control; the eyes to our life force and spirit; the cheekbones to willpower; the forehead to our intellectual capacities; and so on. Every time you meet someone you face-read without realising it.

For the purposes of psychic development, however, it is important to understand that physiognomy is a subjective art and it is the images, feelings and sensations that certain facial features trigger for you that are important. So when you look at someone with thin lips, what does that suggest to you? Don't be tempted to use traditional associations all the time, such as equating a weak chin with a retiring personality. Really look at the person you are studying and make up your own mind.

Hidden in a person's face lies a mood, an energy, and you can become aware of that mood by watching the face move.

The spine

Your spine holds everything together and plays a great part in the upward struggle. To see what messages your spine is capable of sending you, stand with your back straight against a wall. Now take five steps forward and five steps back again, paying close attention to the feelings in the middle of your back. At step four, when you are moving back to the wall, you may become aware of a distinctly different impulse building within your middle and your spine. This feeling signifies that every part of your body, and not just your mind, has the ability to tune into sensations and vibrations around you.

The stomach

Your stomach is an extremely sensitive area. Later on, when you start to use your power to sense other people, you will become highly aware of this area. The term 'gut feeling' is no accident. The area of your body between your heart and your groin, which consists of your stomach and solar plexus, is said by some scientists to have its own intelligence, and some people believe it once had a primitive brain – hence the phrase 'gut feeling'.

Tuning in to your body and the pulsing of life within you is a link to the mystery of life.

The hands, arms and voice

Your hands, arms and voice all perform an extremely complex dance of sound and gesture. The next time you speak to someone, try to concentrate on their hand and arm movements. Can you see patterns? Can you tell what kind of mood they are in?

Some psychics only need to hear a person's voice to gain impressions, so listen carefully to people's tone when they speak to you. Can you tell what they are feeling? You are not so much listening to what other people say; you are tuning into the tone or sounds they use and make. Really listen and try to decipher the emotions floating around in the voice. Even everyday phrases, like 'excuse me' or 'pass the sauce, please', are loaded with emotional undertones. If you are more of a visual person, you may want to close your eyes and listen intently to see how that voice appears in your mind's eye. What shapes, colours or images can you see?

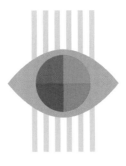

The legs and feet

Think about how you and other people walk – leg movements can speak volumes about a person. Try to copy the way someone else walks; this can bring on powerful feelings of being in tune with that person. And last, but by no means least, your feet are your connection to the earth. Ever heard the phrase 'put yourself in my shoes'? It's amazing how putting on a new pair of shoes can make you feel different and, if you want to understand someone better, just imagine that their shoes are in front of you, and then step into them.

The rest of the body

Being psychic isn't just an experience for your head – it's an experience for your whole body. You can start by feeling your pulse beat. The feeling of your life blood coursing through you with every breath is a link with the great mystery of life. Breathing may seem the simplest thing that you do, but many yogis in the East spend their entire lives trying to get it right – perhaps because breathing is the essence of life. So every time you slow down the pace of your life and concentrate on your breathing alone, you are accessing your most basic self. Keep breathing deeply and the aura may brighten to a colour.

It is easier to build up an image of someone if you place their shoes in front of you – for real or in your mind – and walk in them.

Seeing past the mask

Now that you have started to think of the human body in a psychic way, it is time to try an exercise to help you understand the movements and feelings of others.

1. In much the same way as you did for the people-peeping exercise (see page 61), go to a public spot and look for someone that you can observe without being noticed.

2. This time, instead of imagining what their life might be like, try to imagine that you are them. What would it be like to be that person? What are they feeling? The more you do this exercise, the easier it starts to become to read people accurately. You will be able to see past the masks that people wear.

AURIC SIGHT

Auric sight is the ability to see a subtle energetic field, or aura, that emanates from all physical things. Everything living and non-living has an aura, and the colours and forms of each aura are believed to be characteristic of the person, animal or thing they surround. These shift according to mood and state of health.

Seeing auras

An aura can look like a photographic double-image or a cocoon around a person, life form or object. It can vary in texture, quality and colour. If you want to start seeing auras, you need first to feel as relaxed as possible. Breathe slowly and deeply for a few moments. Then, instead of looking directly at someone, look straight past them and glance casually in their direction, allowing your eyes to lose focus. The aim is to trick your rational mind by putting a lot of concentration on something else, keeping just a vague focus on the person whose aura you want to read. Don't expect people to light up like Christmas trees and stay that way. Visions of auras tend to be lightning-quick, but the more you practise, the more natural it will feel and the more likely it is for the colour to become noticeable.

INTERPRETING AURAS

Once you start to see auras, you can begin to interpret them by thinking about the quality of the colour you are seeing, rather than about the colour itself. Is it clear and bright, or dull and muddy? Is the aura healthy and happy, or are you getting mixed signals? With practise you may begin to link certain shades or colours with emotions.

The colour of a person's aura can tell you an enormous amount about them and their feelings at that moment in time. For example, a person with a happy disposition might have a bright-yellow aura, but this could change to red if that person becomes angry. If someone's aura has dark spots, it could suggest ill health or disturbing emotions. We all interpret colour in different ways, but it helps to have a guide; the list of qualities, given right, is a good starting point. Use it when you practise interpreting auras. Remember, though, that different colours can mean different things to different people. Trust your instinct.

- RED: Survival, strength, motivation, energy, power, anger, change
- ORANGE: Vitality, sexuality, exercise, pleasure, creativity, warmth, passion
- YELLOW: Inspiration, power of the mind, study, ideas, cheerfulness
- GREEN: Nature, balance, harmony, calm, love, compassion
- BLUE: Communication, healing, teaching ability, inspiration, creativity
- INDIGO: Vision, intuition, psychic ability
- VIOLET: Wisdom, enlightenment, spiritual growth
- PINK: Love, warmth, tenderness, youthfulness, nurture, innocence
- GOLD: Love, prosperity, brilliance, creativity
- WHITE: Purity
- BLACK: Depression, crisis, renewal
- BROWN: Practical ability, down-to-earth qualities, solidity, devotion, friendliness

Refocusing your eyes

Developing auric sight is often simply a matter of learning how to refocus your eyes. Normally our eyes are focused on the physical nature of matter, rather than on the subtle energy field around it. This exercise will help you to refocus. The soft light of evening is a good time to do this.

1. Hold your hand about 45 cm (18 in) from your eyes. Look at it, noticing its shapes, lines and texture.

2. Notice the outline of your fingers and thumb as you gently make a fist and then release your hand again.

3. Shift your attention from your hand to something in the distance, such as a picture on the wall. Let your hand remain central, but look through it to your object. Practise shifting your vision back and forth a few times.

4. Notice how different your hand looks as you adjust your focus. Rest your eyes for a moment, then repeat the exercise, but this time leave your eyes focused on the distant object beyond your hand and notice what you see. You might glimpse a small movement of light or energy around your hand or a double-etched image.

TELEPATHY

Telepathy is the mind-to-mind communication of thoughts, feelings and ideas through psychic power. With telepathy there is no need for talking, hand signals or facial expressions – it's all about the power of the mind. If you're telepathic, you can transfer thoughts to another person.

Most of us are telepathic to some degree, but because telepathy is so often combined with body language, we rarely notice it. You may have experienced telepathy if, for instance, you and a friend have the same thought at the same time. Telepathy is more likely to occur when you are very close to someone, such as a friend or relative. Mothers often find that their toddlers answer questions they have only asked in their heads, and telepathy is particularly common among twins and lovers.

Strengthening telepathic connections

Telepathy works best if there are emotions involved. So if you feel really close to someone, why not practise with him or her first. Emotional closeness, or feeling that you are on the same wavelength as someone else, opens psychic channels. Your human friends aren't the only beings who can help you to communicate. Animals have highly developed sensitivities as part of their survival instinct and are extremely sensitive to emotions and subtle changes in the environment. For example, dogs often bark at visitors coming up a path before they've got anywhere near the door. If you have a pet and want to build a strong telepathic bond, you need to spend a lot of time with it first and not try to force the connection. The stronger and happier the bond between you and your pet, the stronger the telepathic communication will be.

Call a friend

Telepathy works best if there is genuine trust and a feeling of safety with another person.

1. Next time you have an internal conversation with someone, give them a call and ask them if they wanted to contact you. You might be surprised at the outcome.

Send yourself a message

Here is another exercise that you might like to try as you discover this amazing ability.

1. Decide on a time when you want to wake up in the morning and visualize waking up at that time, rested and alert. (Hint: you may want to set the alarm, just in case.) Sometimes your inner guide gets stressed out and wakes you in the night or too early in the morning, but after a few attempts you should find that you wake within half an hour of the scheduled time.

TELEPATHIC PARTNERING WORK

The following exercises will help you learn to send and receive information telepathically. The first step is to find a partner – a family member or friend – and give them a try.

Target practice

1. If you keep practising this exercise, you will get a clearer sense of what you are best at: sending or receiving telepathic communication.

2. Select a part of your friend's body as a target. Close your eyes and focus intensely on it. Don't tell your friend what body part you have chosen.

3. Imagine tickling it or patting it for a few moments. Concentrate on feeling the sensation yourself before sending it to your partner.

4. When you have finished sending the information, open your eyes and ask your partner if they felt or thought anything.

5. Switch roles and let your partner target parts of your body in the same way.

Sharpening your telepathic skills

For this exercise you need to agree on a time when you and a friend can sit down to meditate for approximately ten minutes in different locations. You then use the first five minutes to send a message, and the other five minutes to receive a message or the other way around, making sure that your times are synchronized so that one of you receives as the other sends.

1. At the agreed time, start with a few deep breaths and concentrate on sending a message to your friend. Think of the message in whatever way you wish, but stick to a single representation.

2. When the time is up, take a few more deep breaths and shift into receiving mode. Concentrate on opening your mind to the message that your friend is sending.

3. When the exercise is finished, bring yourself back to physical reality and write down everything you can remember about the experience, both in the message you were trying to send and the one you think you received from your friend.

4. Phone or visit each other to compare experiences. How often were you right? How often were you wrong? Don't be discouraged if the results are poor at first; most people improve with practice.

Sending messages to others

This exercise is as simple as sending good thoughts to people you care about. Most of the exercises so far have involved short-distance telepathy, but believe it or not, long-distance telepathy can work too. Remember: negative energy is detrimental to psychic development and will do harm to you, rather than to the person to whom you want to send your thoughts. Thinking good thoughts is therefore essential.

1. Choose someone to whom you'd like to send good thoughts, then find a quiet, comfortable spot and ask that your energy be sent.

2. Now bring that person to mind, and breathe deeply and slowly. As you inhale, see and feel healing light stream into you to heal and bless you. As you exhale, see that wonderful healing energy go from you to the other person to strengthen them.

3. Do this for a few moments. See and feel the other person becoming strong.

4. Offer thanks for the healing and then bring the focus and energy back to you, taking time to see yourself healed and strengthened by the process.

SCANNING PEOPLE

This may sound technical, but it's not. This sort of scanning has nothing to do with computers – it's about seeing the energy and thoughts of others. It may not happen right away, but if you practise the techniques in this chapter every day, you will eventually get the hang of it.

Top to toe

Scanning can tell you a lot about the people you meet.

1. When you are introduced to someone new – a colleague, an employer, whoever – take a moment to imagine that person in a ball of light or pure energy.

2. Now mentally scan that person from top to toe, then from toe to top, noticing any words, images, colours, thoughts or sensations in your body – anything at all (however crazy) that comes up. Remember not to stare; you don't need to look directly at a person to scan them.

3. If you can, write these first impressions down and save them. Once you have got to know the other person better, look back at your notes. Were you right? Did your impressions make sense?

Reading people

It's best to do this exercise initially with someone you know well. When you feel more comfortable with it, you can use it with people you may not know as well.

1. Ask someone you know well to sit opposite you and to keep silent for five minutes. Hold the person's hand and close your eyes. Pay attention to your heart and stomach, noticing what sensations you experience.

2. Breathe deeply and begin to sense information about that other person. Look at their face and their body. Notice any colours that seem to surround them. Take your time – it takes a while for information to filter through. Don't talk or ask any questions; just wait for sensations, thoughts or feelings to pass to you. When you are ready, open your eyes and share the information that you have received. Deliver it as positively as you can.

3. If you have tapped into an area that the person does not feel comfortable discussing, leave it. Instead shift to other impressions that you received.

4. To complete this exercise, move away from the other person and imagine yourself harmlessly breathing out all the feelings that are not yours and that do not belong to you. You should also ground yourself (see page 50) by doing something usual or mundane, such as moving a chair or tidying up.

WORKING
WITH MATTER

By now I hope you are beginning to realize how awesome the power of your mind is.

In this chapter we take things one step further to see how you can actually influence with your thoughts not just people, but also objects, places and situations.

Psychics believe that thoughts can travel outside the body and be absorbed by your environment, and this would indeed account for the sense of atmosphere that you may feel in certain places or situations. For example, the centuries of worship in an ancient church will have imprinted the atmosphere with a vibration of hope; the opposite is true for buildings where violence or tragedy has taken place. The exercises that follow are all designed to help your mind and body become more sensitive to your environment and the objects within it – through energizing your hands, pyschometry and telekinesis – so that you can keep growing and attracting success your way.

TUNE INTO TOUCH

Every day of your life you exchange energy with the people you meet. Without realizing it, you have interacted with the energies coming off the people around you; for example, sometimes you may feel an instant like or dislike for someone without them actually saying a word. Picking up and giving off energy is called imprinting.

When you tune into an object, you're asking your intuition to pass information to you. One way it can do this is by stimulating physical sensations. It may stir up emotions within you or create images in your mind connected to the energy imprints on the object. Here are some ways in which your inner guide can help you receive imprints.

Physical sensations

When you first pick up an object, pay attention to what you feel and where on your body you feel it. You may feel certain physical sensations, such as warmth or coldness. Do you feel an itch, an ache or a tingle? Do you feel tightness anywhere? If you feel tightness in your neck, perhaps the person whose object you are holding is under stress. By relaxing and paying attention to what you feel, you start to connect with the energy imprints on the object. Pay close attention to what you feel and where – you will be amazed at what you discover.

Emotional sensations

Sometimes you may feel strong emotions, such as happiness, sadness or anger, within you as you receive impressions. Usually the emotion you pick up on is the one most recently or most often experienced by the wearer. Don't forget that your intuition can't speak to you in everyday language, and you must find another way to help you understand. So take note of how you are feeling as well as of what you are seeing in your mind's eye.

Visual images

Sometimes your inner guide will help you see things associated with an object. You may see images, colours, people and so on. The hard part isn't seeing the information; it is gaining an understanding of what that information means. If you feel confused, remember that your intuition will always try to use images or thoughts to which you can relate.

Choose objects to tune into that have a history to them, which means those that would have been held or used a lot.

Energizing your hands

This exercise helps to awaken the sensitivities in your hands, so that it becomes easier to use them to feel subtle energies on objects, people and places. Don't worry if you think you are imagining what you sense during this exercise; you are working to recognize subtle energies.

1. Rub the palms of your hands together for about 30 seconds, then extend your hands in front of you, with the palms facing down and about 60 cm (2 ft) apart.

2. Move your hands towards each other, bringing them as close as you can without letting them touch.

3. Now draw your hands slowly back, until they are about 20 cm (8 in) apart. Repeat this in-and-out movement two or three times and, as you do so, pay attention to what you feel. You may sense pressure building between your hands, feel a tickling sensation or sense a warming up or cooling down between your hands.

The next step

After learning to energize your hands and stimulate your sensitivity, you can take things a stage further by energizing your hands and then holding one of them over the forearm of the other. Do you sense any energy surrounding your forearm? Try other parts of your body; get used to sensing your energy field. If you are working with someone else, try sensing their energy field.

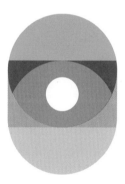

You exchange energy with the people you meet every day.
Picking up and giving off energy is called imprinting.

PSYCHOMETRY

Your aura is your own personal energy imprint, but as we have seen, energy exchange doesn't just occur between people; it can also occur between plants, places, animals and objects.

The longer and more direct your contact with something, the greater the imprint you will leave; watches and wedding rings, for example (because they are worn every day), tend to have powerful imprints. Psychics believe that furniture, clothing, jewellery and even the walls of a building all hold vibrational, or 'residual' energy. Reading the energy imprints on things and places is a psychic technique called psychometry.

Psychometry can be a useful way of picking up information about something or somewhere. Information held in objects can be good, bad or indifferent. For example, if you pick up a bride's wedding veil, you might feel the excitement of the day.

Sensing the colour of a card

In this exercise you are going to try and sense the colour of the suits without looking at the cards. Red cards have a different energy and feel to black cards.

1. Get a pack of playing cards, then energize your hands (see page 104).

2. Place one black card in front of you and turn it face up. Place your hands over it, close your eyes and pay attention to what you feel. Do the same with a red card.

3. Now spread out the whole pack face down and choose a card. Keep it face down and try to feel if it is black or red. Turn the card over and see if you were correct; repeat with another card. You will be surprised at how quickly you improve.

Guess what?

The best way to develop psychometry, or indeed any psychic ability, is to practise. Here is an exercise you might like to try with other people.

1. Ask some of your friends to bring some small objects, then place them in envelopes so that you have no idea which object belongs to whom.

2. Now energize your hands (see page 104).

3. Choose an envelope and take the object out.

4. Close your eyes and relax. Try to attune yourself to the object in your hands by paying attention to any physical, emotional and visual sensations (see pages 102–3) that come to you. Start with the physical sensations. Do you feel hot, cold, itchy? Does a part of your body tingle or appear before your mind? Next, concentrate on your emotions. Finally, concentrate on whatever images come to mind.

5. When you have finished sensing everything, write down all your impressions on the envelope and share your experience with the owner of the object. Get as much detail and feedback as you can, and don't worry if you get things wrong – it isn't a contest.

SENSING ATMOSPHERES

Just as objects have their own energy and feel, so everything that happens in an object's environment affects it and can be registered by those with psychic – and in particular clairsentient – ability. You may, for example, like or dislike the way a room or a place looks or smells; this is because part of you is picking up on its energy imprint or atmosphere.

A room or place that is loved and cared for will feel quite different from a room that is neglected, or from one in which shocking, violent or tragic events have taken place. There is also a difference between a room that is used by people who relate well to each other and one in which there are arguments and bitterness.

Psychics can balance the energies in a room in a similar way to Feng Shui practitioners; a plant can help to transform the feeling of a room.

HARMONIZING THE ENVIRONMENT

Feng Shui experts know a great deal about the need to balance energies in an environment, because they believe that a balanced environment becomes a healthier and happier place for people to live and work in. Psychics work in a similar way, but rather than following a particular system, such as Feng Shui, their intuition tells them how to bring harmony to their surroundings. They may suggest healing colours, shapes or objects, such as a fish tank or a plant, that can transform the feeling of an environment.

A drop in the ocean

This exercise is a fantasy meditation designed to stimulate your environmental awareness.

1. Sit or lie down comfortably, either in your sacred space (see pages 46–7) or in another quiet atmosphere.

2. Breathe deeply and imagine yourself to be a beautiful tropical fish in an ocean. Enjoy the feeling of freedom as you glide through the water.

3. Now imagine yourself to be a fish amid a school of brightly coloured fish. You swim in rhythm with the group. You sense its mood, and shift your direction in perfect time and rhythm with the others.

4. Take this one step further and imagine yourself able to feel the mood of the entire ocean. You automatically sense where to feed, play and swim, and where you will be safe. You are in total harmony with your underwater world. Wouldn't it be amazing if you could sense, read and respond to the physical environment in which you live and work in just this way?

Sensing places

In this exercise you will think about the places in your life where you spend a lot of time – home, work, the car – in order to help you observe your impressions of the world around you.

1. Write down the places where you spend most of your time.

2. Consider what places leave you with a good impression? What places leave you feeling unsettled? Think about which places are good for you and which aren't. You may discover that certain rooms in your house, or sections of a particular road, are not as good as others. You don't need to give a reason why, or look for any cause.

3. Once you have made your observations, you may want to talk to a friend about them. You may be surprised how often other people feel the same way, for no apparent reason.

Getting to know a room

This exercise is designed to help you detect feelings and atmospheres around you right now.

1. Walk around the room you are in, or go to another room in your house (not your bedroom).

2. How light or dark is it? What colours are in it? What shapes? How warm or cold is it? What sounds do you hear? What does it smell like?

3. Now put your hand on your stomach and notice how you feel about this room. Is the area relaxed or tense? Does the room have a personality? Is there a happy atmosphere? Are the people who use this room happy, or is there some stress? Has anything happened in the past in this room to influence the present?

4. Trust your gut instincts to give you the answers. If the room doesn't feel balanced, ask yourself what needs to change to improve the atmosphere so that your feelings might be better. You could do this by rearranging the furniture, hanging pictures on the walls or inviting more positive people and experiences into your room.

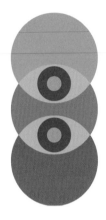

Keep practising

As you do these exercises, you may want to take note of your impressions and compare them with those you have in the same location at another time. Remember, the best results come from practice, and it certainly is worth practising, because the ability to tune into the energies of atmospheres, objects and people can help keep you safe. If you have a gut feeling that something isn't safe or right, or that someone isn't to be trusted, make sure you listen to it.

CLEANSING A ROOM

Throughout history, people have used ritual and ceremony to cleanse the energy from their environment, to create a sacred space. Rooms collect the energies that are expressed in them because in the course of daily life we experience and share a multitude of emotions. During times of stress you can walk into a room and be greeted, not with a feeling of warmth and comfort, but with feelings of fatigue, apathy and even depression.

Ceremony and ritual can help focus and intensify our energies and many people believe the power comes from the intent and belief of the person who is performing or experiencing the ceremony. The ritual used to create a sacred space may be as simple as visualizing white light to dispel darkness or lighting a candle to burn away negative energies. Using a singing bowl creates an uplifting and cleansing sound, which raises the vibrations of a room. However, it may take decades and the energy of many thousands of people to create a sacred place, like the building of great temples or the Great Pyramids of Egypt.

TELEKINESIS

Telekinesis (derived from the ancient Greek words for 'distant movement') is the ability to move objects using thoughts and energy alone. It is also known as psychokinesis or PK (from the ancient Greek for 'mind movement'), and can additionally mean changing the shape of an object or transporting it from one place to another, using the power of the mind or body energy.

This amazing psychic phenomenon has been reported throughout the ages. Uri Geller came to public attention in the 1970s with his ability to bend spoons and other objects using mind-power alone. How does this intriguing phenomenon work, and is it possible to learn this skill?

How telekinesis works

One theory put forward to explain telekinesis is that the concentration of the energy from a person's mind somehow alters the energy structure of the object on which it is focused. When the mind's stream of energy is released, the object reforms itself according to the energy patterns being created. If someone has sent 'bending' energy, the object bends; if they have sent 'floating' energy, the object floats.

Developing telekinesis

Many people discover their gift for telekinesis after a serious illness or accident, and there are numerous reports of people being able to move objects, see the future and even read minds following near-death experiences. For some reason, being hurt or ill seems to tap into hidden human abilities and activate them.

Telekinesis is not an easy power to develop, and the great majority of people would benefit more from investing their energies in other areas of psychic development. Having said that, who knows what someone is capable of, given the right practice? It is vital to note that if you don't accept that you have the potential to harness the power of telekinesis, your mind will work against you.

Uri Geller's telekinetic powers have made him famous all over the world.

Moving small items

The idea of being able to make large, heavy objects fly around the room – like Harry Potter or a Jedi Knight – is magical, but the reality is not quite so dramatic. Small, light objects, such as pieces of paper or pins, are far more likely to be moved using this skill, so try with these first.

1. Energize your hands according to the guidelines already given (see page 104).

2. Place them near a small object, such as a little piece of kitchen foil or a used match. Cup your hands around the item until you can sense the edge of its energy.

3. Once you can feel this, try to visualize the energy flowing from your hands into the item, and imagine moving it with this energy. Be patient, for it takes time to build and release the energy in the right way for the object to respond.

4. Practise for a few minutes every day. If you keep practising, in time the object may move or twitch – this is your telekinetic influence on it. Keep doing this exercise with different types of objects in different environments.

THOUGHT FORMS

Thought forms are emotions and thoughts created in the mind, but not in the physical brain. They are transmitted by means of auric energy fields. Psychics see them as whirling objects in a person's aura. Telekinesis is the power of the mind over matter using thought forms to create psychic phenomena, while telepathy is the transmission of thought forms directly into the mind of another.

Psychics believe that most of us find that success and fulfilment are elusive because we focus on working towards our goals through physical action, rather than manifesting them through our inner vision. However, when we focus our full attention on what we desire, we fuel the creation of thought forms that attract what we want into our lives. In short, the more we focus or concentrate on a particular goal, the stronger its potential becomes. Through the process of repeating a thought or maintaining a focus, we actually create a thought form that becomes self-sustaining and draws what we want into our lives.

Thoughts have the power to attract whatever we want into our lives.

Creating thought forms

To do this exercise you need first to define your goal. It doesn't matter what it is, but it is essential that you believe your dream is possible. If you don't, aim a little lower until your goal no longer feels out of reach. It is also important that your goal does not involve harming or hurting someone else in any way.

1. Set aside about a half an hour for this exercise. You need to be able to sit quietly without interruptions of any sort. Make sure you feel comfortable, relaxed and in a positive frame of mind, because the more positive your state of mind, the more effective you will be.

2. Sit down and close your eyes. Visualize a whirlpool of universal energy swirling around you. Feel the energy growing stronger, and see it moving and flashing with radiant and vibrant colours. This ball of energy is going to channel creative power and energy to you.

3. As you see yourself at the centre of this ball of energy, clearly visualize your goal coming true. Hold a mental image of success, and imagine as deeply as possible how it will feel to attain it. Imagine what you might say or hear, what you might do or where you might be. Try to make this visualization as 'real' as possible. The more powerfully you can imagine success, the better.

4. Affirm to yourself that what you desire is not only possible, but is already in the process of manifesting itself and ready to become real.

5. When you are ready, imagine the whirlpool of energy melting into you and back into the universe. Give thanks to the energy and slowly open your eyes. Walk away with the belief that the energy within you will keep growing and attracting success.

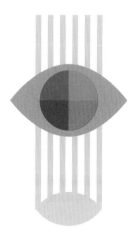

WORKING
WITH TIME

Now that you are working to develop your psychic abilities by exploring the power of your subconscious mind over yourself, other people and the world you live in, you are ready to get to grips with psychic abilities that are 'time-based'. This may be the area of psychic development that first caught your imagination. It is definitely the most sensational, as it includes looking into the future, knowing the past and understanding the present.

As you work through this chapter, bear in mind that your intuition talks to you about your past, present and future through whatever form of psychic communication is easiest for you to understand.

Some will sense, visualize or dream about the future; others will use divination tools, such as colour divination, a crystal ball, Tarot cards or tea-leaf reading, to help them understand what is going on with their lives and to solve problems. Whichever way you choose to communicate, it is important to understand that each time you reach out to your subconscious power, your connection to it will grow stronger and you will increase your psychic ability.

UNDERSTANDING THE FUTURE

Keep in mind that you create possible futures for yourself because of what you decide to do or not do in your life. For example, you are more likely to pass a driving test if you decide to take driving lessons than if you don't. You create possibilities in the future through choices and actions in the present.

So, in many ways you can see into your future by recognizing the patterns of behaviour that set you up for success or failure. The key is to be able to recognize these patterns, and the best way to do that is to establish a strong connection with your intuition by working through the exercises in this book.

Shaping your future

Your intuition can help you see what is more likely to happen in your future if you follow a certain course of action or behave in a certain way. This is because your subconscious recognizes that all things are connected and that every action has an equal and opposite reaction. Everything you do and think sets energy into motion and shapes your future. The trick is to figure out how things relate to each other and how one act can lead to another.

Your intuition can also help you create a better future for yourself by showing you that you have the power to choose. There will always be things that happen to you that you can't possibly predict, but you can use your intuition to discern probable outcomes and effect changes that will make these outcomes more favourable to you.

The future is not set in stone, but as the Buddhist Wheel of Life shows, every action has an equal and opposite action.

Is the future set in stone?

No, the future is only probable, which means that it is changeable. However, if a psychic says something will happen and nothing is done to alter the course, then that outcome will most likely occur. For example, a psychic may see someone getting ill because of poor lifestyle choices; that person can then choose to ignore that vision or change their habits.

Can we mould our own future? Absolutely. This is why many psychics don't like to tell people what they will be doing in the future, because that is up to them. Most of your future is determined by your own attitudes, choices, personal programming and self-limiting (or unlimited) beliefs. Instead of telling you about your 'probable' future, it's much better to help you create an amazing future – which anyone can have, including you.

Psychics can predict possible futures but whether they become a reality is up to you and the choices you make.

DIVINATION TOOLS

An important part of working with your sixth sense is learning to use divination tools. They can act as bridges to your inner guide, providing you with wisdom, understanding and insight. It may help to think of them as a kind of high-speed modem that gives you greater and quicker access to the information and knowledge on the web of your subconscious powers.

If you are a beginner in psychic-development work, divination tools can be really helpful because they give you something concrete to work with and a framework in which to test your intuition. In time, you may find that you don't need to use these tools, because you have established a strong connection with your psychic powers and can draw on them at any time, anywhere. Until then, you may want to explore and learn to use several tools, finding out which works best for you in understanding and interpreting messages from your higher self.

Crystals can be very effective psychic tools if you have an affinity for working with them.

Interpreting images

In the pages that follow, some of the many divination tools that can help you tap into the psychic part of yourself will be discussed. As you experiment with them in the days, weeks and months ahead, remember that your intuition usually communicates through symbols, sensations and images. Your task is to figure out what these feelings, pictures and symbols mean.

While you can of course go out and buy a standard dictionary of symbols, don't forget that all images have a personal dimension, and each of them has a meaning that is unique to you. For example, the image of a dog may be a sign of companionship to some people, but if you are frightened of dogs it could equally be a symbol of menace. Your intuition knows this and will use your personal associations when it presents images to you. So always begin with what the image means to you, before exploring standard or common interpretations. Ask yourself simple questions like 'How does this make me feel' or 'How does it fit into my life now?'

Cloud-gazing

One of the simplest and oldest forms of divination is cloud-reading. It was commonly practised by the Celts (particularly the Druids), who determined fortunes by looking at the formations and movements of clouds.

Why not go outside now, or look out of the window, and let your imagination try to make sense of the shapes you see in the clouds? Don't stare intently at them (or at the sun); just look at them softly, with the kind of gentle gaze you would have if you were daydreaming. Think about a question and, as you look at the clouds, pay attention to their shapes. Your imagination will help you recognize images that relate to your particular issue. What do those images mean to you? How do they make you feel? Trust your imagination and intuition to help you see what applies to your question. Remember: you will see and feel what your intuition knows you can relate to.

With every cloud divination you will strengthen your ability to connect with your intuition and thereby develop your psychic power. You also have a tool that you can use for as long as there are clouds in the sky.

Cloud watching is a wonderful way to practise understanding your higher mind.

COLOUR DIVINATION

Colour-reading is a divination tool you can use anywhere and at any time you choose. Many people believe that, when dressing, we subconsciously choose colours that we think will help us throughout the day. Your intuition directs you to these hues because colours express energy, and each colour has its own unique quality. Remember, though, that the way you interpret colours is unique to you.

Sometimes people choose to wear or surround themselves with a colour that is opposite to the way they feel or what they are doing, in order to balance out something about themselves. For example, if you have been studying or working hard, you may find that you are drawn to orange, the colour of fun, creativity and vitality.

Begin to get into the habit of looking at colours as a reflection of a person's mood or character. Ask yourself if the shade they are wearing is a revealing or a balancing colour. Trust your impressions on this. In time you will be able to recognize basic qualities and moods in people by the colours they wear. You will then have insights into other people, no matter how they present themselves. You will also be able to start choosing colours that can help you strengthen and balance yourself. For instance, if you need to be calm, wear blue; if you need to feel energetic, wear red; and so on.

COLOUR GUIDE

- BLACK: Often considered a negative colour, it is in fact a sign of movement and transition from one phase to another, or of rest before the beginning of a new day. It is also the colour of quiet strength, protection and stability.
- BLUE: The colour of loyalty, truth and justice, as well as teamwork, calm and harmony. On the dark side, it can be a sign of being too deeply involved in one thing at the expense of others.
- BROWN: A down-to-earth and practical colour of devotion and loyalty. On the dark side, it can indicate being overly harsh or critical.
- GOLD: A symbol of success and achievement, as well as wealth.
- GREEN: The colour of honesty, healing, balance, peace, hope and new beginnings. Less positively, it might suggest the phrase 'green with envy', or the phrase 'green as grass', suggesting a need to grow up and take more responsibility.
- ORANGE: A rejuvenating colour of fun and creativity, and a sign of confidence, encouraging you to believe in yourself and go for it.
- PINK: The colour of simplicity, peace and happiness.
- RED: Traditionally the colour of power, strength and energy, it can also reflect strong emotions, such as passionate love and anger.
- SILVER: The colour of intuition and romance.

- VIOLET AND PURPLE: These colours indicate intelligence and high principles. Violet is a colour of sensitivity and noble ideals, and purple is a colour of positive transformation.
- WHITE: Suggestive of fresh starts, inspiration and illumination; if there is no other colour with the white, it can suggest loneliness and isolation.
- YELLOW: The colour of light, laughter and creativity, but also associated with cowardice or exhaustion.

The next time you choose or buy clothes, let your intuition guide you to the colours that will be of most benefit to you.

SCRYING AND CRYSTAL-GAZING

The crystal ball is the classic and best-known method of divination. Many assume the crystal ball has the power, but this isn't the case. The secret lies in the technique of scrying.

Scrying is a mental process, like cloud-gazing. The difference is that when you scry you don't need to find shapes – you just see things. Traditionally a crystal ball is used in scrying, but you don't have to use one. Some psychics can scry on any surface they choose, such as a mirror, a bowl of water or even their fingernails. However, when you begin scrying you may want to use a quartz crystal and/or a bowl of water. Quartz crystals emit a form of electrical energy that helps stimulate psychic powers, and water has a magical and mystical power. You can find quartz crystals in any New Age store, and it doesn't matter what shape a crystal is or how it is marked; one that fits snugly into your palm is good to start with.

Simple scrying exercise

With every attempt at scrying you strengthen your ability, and in time the images you see will become clearer.

1. Begin with slow, rhythmic breathing, and place your hands around a crystal or a bowl of water.

2. Focus on what the problem is or on what you want to know. As you hold or touch the crystal or bowl of water, feel it coming to life. Imagine that energy is growing within you.

3. Stay relaxed and pay attention to the formations you see in the crystal or bowl – watch how the light reflects or catches. Don't stare too hard; just look softly.

4. Your intuition will help you recognize images that relate to your question. Ask yourself what they mean to you. You will see clouds appearing and disappearing, and you may even catch glimpses of the future. Your state of mind when scrying will need to be calm and focused.

TAROT CARDS

At first glance the Tarot seems really complicated, but in essence the cards are simply triggers for your intuition. You don't need to understand the history and complex symbolism of the cards to work with them or use them as divination tools; you just need to pay attention to what feelings the cards inspire in you. The deck consists of 78 cards divided into two groups: the minor arcana (56 cards) and the major arcana (22 cards). There are four suits in each park: pentacles, swords, cups and wands. It might help to think of Tarot cards as picture books for adults. The experience is completely visual, and the cards' purpose is to inspire feelings inside you.

Which deck to choose

If you're looking for a deck, try the Rider-Waite deck, as it is probably the best one to start with. For the time being, just take a look at some of the pictures in your deck, if you have one. Fan your cards out in front of you. You will see before you a blaze of shapes, images, signs and symbols, composed of flowers, weapons, animals, monsters, angels and planets. Pay attention to the way the cards make you feel. Look at the pictures in a quiet, reflective manner. Hold on to these feelings for a moment. Emotional reactions to the pictures are a sign that the Tarot cards are working their magic – they are getting through to your psychic centre via your imagination.

Using Tarot as a divination tool

Typically, Tarot cards are read by shuffling and then laying out the cards, face down in various formations or spreads. Each position in the spread is thought to have a particular meaning and significance, and each major- or minor-arcana card laid down has an individual meaning. Most people who use the Tarot believe it should not be read for definitive 'yes' or 'no' answers to questions, but for a reflection of existing energies and directions concerning a situation. In other words, the Tarot is good for helping someone see their life from a new perspective, and for indicating the likely outcome of events if things continue as they are at present.

Although spreads are most commonly used for divinatory purposes, results can also be achieved by analysing just one card picked at random. In fact, some people like to draw a single card at the start of each day and meditate on it, to trigger their intuitive powers.

A E Waite (1857–1942) produced the 78 card deck, known as the Rider-Waite deck, that we still use today.

The touchstone spread

Touchstone means a point of reference. Using the touchstone spread is a great way to get to know the cards one at a time.

1. At the beginning of each day, spread out all the cards face down.

2. Then choose one at random, using it as a reference point for the events that lie ahead that day.

3. At the end of the day reflect on what has happened, and how the Tarot card you picked either summed up or provided a commentary on these events.

OTHER METHODS OF DIVINATION

In addition to Tarot cards, there are many other types of divination tool to help you awaken and connect to your sixth sense. It would be impossible to mention them all, but here are some tools that are commonly used by psychics to gain greater insight into their past, present and future.

Popular divination tools

- ASTROLOGY: Studies the stars and planets to see how their movements affect your life.
- NUMEROLOGY: Pursues the idea that everything in the universe is based on mathematics. By interpreting the numbers contained in names and birth dates, life paths and potentials can be revealed.
- PENDULUMS AND DIVINING RODS: These form a bridge between the external reality of electrical impulses and the inner self. Interpreting the movement of the pendulum or rods can provide answers to questions.
- BIBLIOMANCY: Involves thinking about a particular problem or question, then randomly taking a book off a bookshelf and opening it at any page. Most of the time the page to which you turn can offer you some form of guidance or new insights.
- THE I CHING: Like Tarot cards and runes, the I Ching uses symbols and patterns to provide insights into problems, and to help you understand and interpret significant events in your life.

INTERPRETING DREAMS

Every time you go to bed and drift off to sleep, you cross a mysterious threshold of consciousness. To develop your psychic awareness further, you need to become fully aware of your entire existence – including the time you spend sleeping.

Dreams can help us make sense of what happened during the day, enabling us to understand what may be bothering us. They can aid in solving problems, present opportunities to play out our desires, and confront our fears. They can also use scenarios to communicate messages about our past, present and future.

Interpreting your dreams

Some of the images that come to you in your dreams may be universally recognized – a boat, for example, is typically a symbol of transition – but most can only be interpreted by you. Relate to your dream as if it were a person who is suddenly found in your home; you must find out who it is and what it wants. Ask it questions like these:

- Are you highlighting mistakes I have made (or am likely to make)?
- Are you showing me my fears?
- Are you telling me to make changes?

Free association

A good way to uncover the meaning of your dreams is by free association: simply go with the first thing that pops into your mind. For instance, if you dreamed of a cat, what are your first thoughts when you think of cats? The more you work with your dreams, the more familiar you will become with your personal images. In the often surreal world of dreams there is no place for logic, and the answer to your question may feature in your dream even before the question has been raised.

Your dream diary

Sadly, many of us forget our dreams on waking and this is a great loss. According to the Talmud, 'A dream which is not interpreted is like a letter which is not read'. Unless written down immediately on waking, most dreams fade within a few minutes, so it is crucial to capture them in a dream diary as soon as you can. Immediately on waking, write down your dream or dreams – even if it's the middle of the night. The process of recording them in words will create a permanent record to which you can refer later, to help you figure out what it is that your subconscious is trying to communicate to you.

In your dream diary, try to include the date, any people involved, the moods and feelings expressed, prominent colours, numbers or shapes, conflicts encountered, dominant symbols or stories, the dream landscape and whether it was past, present or future; and, finally, how the dream ended.

Dream incubation

You can turn your dreams into creative experiences by a process called dream incubation, where you get your waking mind to work with your sleeping mind to help you solve problems in your waking life.

1. Decide what you want to dream about, what problem you want to resolve or what question you want to be answered. Write down your question or desired dream on a piece of paper. Be as specific as you can.

2. Read this over and over again during the day, and again as you get ready for bed.

3. Once in bed, read the question again and ask your dreaming self to bring you the answer during sleep. Put the paper under your pillow or near your bed.

4. Tell yourself before you go to sleep that you will have the dream you asked for, and trust that you will.

5. Tell yourself you will remember your dream. Be prepared to write it down when you wake up and be open to whatever comes to you.

6. Leave your dream intention to incubate. Relax your mind before you sleep. Be willing to experiment and try again if necessary.

LUCID DREAMING

A lucid dream is one in which you are aware that you are dreaming while you are actually dreaming. This can help you interpret the meaning of your dreams, find solutions to problems, work through emotional issues and promote physical and mental healing. Many believe that lucid dreaming is a step towards a form of enlightenment.

To use this technique you need to form a habit, in waking life, of asking yourself 'Am I dreaming or awake?' every time you encounter some common stimulus, such as getting dressed or sneezing. Sooner or later you will encounter the same stimulus in your dream. If you ask the question while dreaming, you'll probably figure out that you are asleep.

The best dream dictionary there is, is the one that is written by you.

Solving problems through lucid dreams

With lucid dreaming it may be possible to access the creativity of your dreaming mind intentionally to help solve problems in your waking life.

1. Before you go to bed, decide on a problem you would like to solve. Frame it as a question, such as 'How can I be more confident?'.

2. Write your question down, memorize it and keep going over and over it in your mind before you go to sleep.

3. Visualize yourself looking for the answer in your dreams. Then, if you fall asleep and become aware that you are dreaming, explore your dream world with your question in mind. Look for any clues that might suggest an answer, even seeking out advice from other characters in your dreams. For example, if you aren't feeling well, dreaming in green will help get your body's natural healing process started.

Precognitive dreams

Carl Jung, the great Swiss analytical psychologist, believed that the unconscious could manifest itself through dreams or premonitions. Often these intrusions are of a personal nature, commenting on the current life experience or situation of the dreamer, but there are times when the dreaming mind might offer glimpses of the future. Such dreams are called 'precognitive dreams'. For instance, you may dream of a friend being involved in an accident, only to discover a week later that this has actually happened, when your friend calls to say she has broken her leg.

Precognitive dreams have been reported throughout history; famous examples are the Pharaoh's dream of seven fat and seven thin cows, and Bishop Lanyi's dream of the assassination of Archduke Franz Ferdinand, which triggered the First World War.

Though they are generally considered symbolic of psychological processes, some precognitive dreams and nightmares are intended as guidance or warnings on a practical level. For instance, if you were to dream about the brakes failing on your car, it might help to ponder whether you are figuratively having trouble 'slowing yourself down' in life; it wouldn't hurt, however, to actually check the brakes on your car in waking life.

In the majority of cases, dreams about disasters or death are not actual predictions, but symbolic representations of current trends of behaviour, courses of action or decisions, which may be detrimental to the health or well-being of the people in question unless they are changed. There are rare occasions when a dream does appear to predict accurately a future event (usually an everyday event). How and why this occurs is unknown, but if it does occur to you it certainly indicates potential psychic ability.

TRAVELLING IN TIME

Surprisingly, we all have the ability to see or sense the future. You have probably already done so: for example, when you get a hunch that something is going to happen and it does, when you hear the phone ring and know who is calling, when you switch on your computer and know how many emails will be waiting, or when you visit an unfamiliar place and get a sense of déjà vu – the feeling that you have been there before. You just need to believe in your powers of precognition.

Precognition

Precognition is the ability to see into the future through dreams and daytime impressions. In other words, it is knowing the unknowable and seeing the unseen; it is knowing how something will happen at some time in the future, either the far or near future.

The most widely held belief is that precognition offers a glimpse of a possible future that is based on current conditions and information, one that can be altered depending upon acts of free choice. Some researchers have tried to explain precognition by proposing that it is possible to detach yourself from the linear flow of time – when, at a given moment, we are at one point on a continuum linking past, present and future – to another temporal plane where points in the past and the future can be observed. Another theory is that precognitive experiences unleash powerful telekinetic energy (see page 144) that helps create the future. In other words, your promotion at work becomes a self-fulfilling prophecy, because if you believe something sufficiently strongly, it tends to happen.

Premonition may be difficult to understand, but the conscious knowledge that precognition exists and is a real possibility is the most important step towards developing it. The best form of development exercise for precognition is to work on the divination skills mentioned previously, such as Tarot cards (see pages 135–6), scrying (see pages 133–4), reading tea leaves (see page 27) or indeed any form of concentration that enables you to see into the future.

The Celtic Cross spread of Tarot cards can provide lots of detail to help predict the future.

The Psychic News

The best time to do this exercise is in the evening, because the more relaxed you are, the more accurate predictions tend to be; the subconscious mind also tends to be more active the closer you are to sleep.

1. Sit in an upright chair, close your eyes and do some deep breathing.

2. When you feel relaxed enough, let your mind drift; but don't fall asleep. You need to retain a state between sleeping and waking.

3. Watch your thoughts, but don't follow them. Be the observer of yourself and think in pictures, not words. For example, if you think, 'I must do the grocery shopping tomorrow', convert this into a picture – see the shopping basket, the fruit and the vegetables.

4. Now imagine a blank newspaper in front of you, with only the name Psychic News in position as the masthead. Start to transfer the images of your current thoughts on to the blank white pages. You are triggering your precognition by encouraging your subconscious mind to associate the images it throws up with future headlines.

5. Visualize the images changing to printed words. Try to pick up one or two words. The toughest part of this exercise is understanding what you have seen. Your first results may be disappointing, but keep trying – the more you believe in yourself, the closer you will come to achieving results. It takes time to learn to shift your centre of consciousness, but it is possible if you believe in yourself and focus on your future.

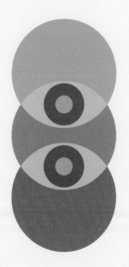

LOOKING FORWARD AND BACK

Nobody really understands what time is; even scientists are confused. As you read this book, time is continuously passing, and all you can be fairly sure of is that the present moment exists. But do the future and the past possess the same reality as the present? Is the passing of time an illusion?

Eastern mystics, including Buddhist monks, stress the importance of living in the 'Eternal Now'. They are continually aware of levels of existence that are beyond the mind and impossible to grasp with thinking. If we could comprehend the Eternal Now, we would understand the meaning of the past and see the blueprint of the future. In other words, our relationship to the past and future is determined by our present state of consciousness, changing according to our state of mind. If we feel positive and happy, the past seems insignificant and the future optimistic; but if we feel gloomy, the past can seem heavy and the future bleak. Therefore if we appreciate and value the present, we free ourselves from the tyranny of time. And if a dream or precognitive vision gives you a glimpse of the future, remember that the future is flexible. You can change it by changing your mind.

Tomorrow is another day

This exercise will help you think about the future – you may even make a prediction or two.

1. Choose a comfortable place where you can concentrate your thoughts.

2. Close your eyes, breathe deeply and be sure that your feet are firmly planted on the floor.

3. Take a few breaths, then project yourself into the next day. See yourself following through your plans for tomorrow. See, hear, feel and taste what your day will be like. Take your time.

4. When you have finished, jot down some notes about what you noticed and saw. What were you wearing? What were you doing? What did you hear? How did you feel? What did you smell?

5. Save your notes and read them over the following night to see how accurate your predictions were.

The Buddhist Wheel of Life illustrates the teachings of Buddhism, such as the cycle of birth, life and death.

Looking back

According to the world's oldest religions – Hinduism and Buddhism – everyone has lived numerous past lives and will probably live many more; ideally, we all learn and improve through each lifetime. The concept of 'karma' (the Sanskrit word for 'act' or 'action') holds that whether good or bad karma comes your way – you can learn lessons from it and grow spiritually. In fact, certain schools of thought believe that a lifetime filled with obstacles triggers the learning of greater lessons.

The ability to recall past lives with our normal consciousness is quite elusive, which is why ancient sages suggest that we increase our awareness and practise yoga. Past-life recall may also occur in dreams, in clairsentient experiences when visiting certain places, and in irrational fears of specific activities. It may also explain why you feel drawn to a particular location, country or culture, why you sometimes meet people you instantly like or dislike for no apparent reason, and why some skills or knowledge come more naturally to you than others.

SYNCHRONICITY

Have you ever found yourself in exactly the right place at the right time? Has the phone ever rung with an answer to a question exactly when you most needed it? Many people brush such common experiences aside as mere coincidences, but there is nothing insignificant about them. They are examples of synchronicity.

What is synchronicity?

Webster's Dictionary describes synchronicity as a coincidence of events that appear to be meaningfully related. But it is really easy to overlook synchronicity – it happens so naturally and subtly in our lives that you may not even notice it.

The father of analytical psychology, Carl Jung, coined the term 'synchronicity' to describe 'a causal connecting principle that links mind and matter'. He believed that the subconscious attracts meaningful coincidences, and that an underlying connectedness that cannot be explained logically draws everything and everyone together with a sense that there is something bigger out there – something that seems to have our best interests at heart.

All the divination techniques to which you have been introduced in this chapter are based on the principle of synchronicity. The fall of coins or cards is connected with a random event, and this random event takes on a special meaning. As you start to work with the exercises in this book, you will not only begin to hear your intuition; you will also be able to recognize the signs of synchronicity.

Developing synchronicity

Until you gain confidence in your ability to pick up the subtle clues of synchronicity, here are a few more exercises to help you tune in.

- As you're waking up in the morning, see if you can get any impressions of the day's news headlines before you hear or read them.
- Before you turn on the radio, see if you can guess what music will be playing.
- Next time you are at a bank of lifts, see if you can guess which one is going to arrive next.
- When you are at the supermarket checkout, try to guess which queue is going to be fastest.

A higher force?

Are forces like synchronicity simply a matter of coincidence, luck or chance, or is something else involved? Perhaps you already believe in a higher force or divine purpose. Or perhaps you don't believe in any other order at all. Whatever your beliefs, if you stay alert and aware, you may just notice that synchronicity plays a much bigger part in your life than you previously imagined.

Most forms of divination, including Tarot cards, are based on the idea of synchronicity. Let your intuition guide you in deciding if the fall of the cards is random or meaningful.

WORKING
WITH OTHER
DIMENSIONS

In this chapter you will learn how to develop skills to see beyond physical barriers to other locations, and – for those who believe there is more to this life than merely material reality – how to experience other dimensions of existence. First we look at remote viewing, or the ability to see in your mind's eye an object or person who is in a different place or even a different time from you. Then you will be travelling to the different levels of consciousness that psychics believe each person possesses, by means of astral projection and out-of-body experiences. We also discuss the possibility of encountering angels and spirit guides on your mental travels.

Within you is someone of great potential and wisdom
– someone who is developing your psychic power.

Within you is your inner voice, sometimes called your spirit guide, higher self, inner guide or creative spark. Most people keep their higher self hidden away deep within themselves, but with every psychic-development exercise you have done so far in this book, and will do in this chapter, it is becoming stronger and more powerful in your daily life.

REMOTE VIEWING

Remote viewing is the psychic ability to witness events, objects or locations beyond the range of the human eye. For example, a viewer might be asked to describe a location on the other side of the world, which they have never visited; an event that happened long ago; or an object sealed in a container or locked in a room; or perhaps even to describe a person or an activity – all without being told anything about the target (not even its name or designation).

Origins

Remote viewing has been reported for centuries but the term itself was coined in the 1970s by American physicists Russell Targ and Harold Puthoff. They set up a remote-viewing research project at Stanford Research Institute in California and conducted hundreds of experiments over a period of ten years. They came to the conclusion that remote viewing is a psychic experience that occurs naturally in people, but is also a skill that can be learned, after finding that they could train people to remote-view regardless of psychic ability. For example, people could be taught to 'see' into a container to describe the objects inside.

In 1972, during the height of the Cold War, the American CIA launched a classified project to train and utilize psychic spies, and the remote-viewing project based at the Stanford Research Institute was a direct response to the USSR's similar training of military personal for long-distance spying. The CIA project operated surreptitiously for 24 years, under codenames as such STAR GATE, SUN STREAK and CENTER LANE, before it was declassified and terminated in 1995.

Research operations in remote viewing continue today, and both scientists and psychics alike remain intrigued by the possibilities it can offer. According to the International Remote Viewing Association (www.irva.org), remote viewing is not really a 'psychic phenomenon' as such, but is actually an imposed discipline or skill that helps the viewer facilitate or harness their own innate, underlying intuitive abilities. Its use certainly transcends detective work or espionage.

Someone with remote viewing skills can harness their intuitive ability to visualize a scene like this without ever seeing it before.

Remote-viewing exercise

Try remote viewing for yourself with this simple exercise.

1. Choose a place that you wish to visit, but haven't yet been to, and about which you know very little. If you are with a friend, you could choose something like their office, or a relative's home.

2. After choosing your 'target', get comfortable and relaxed, and close your eyes. Take several breaths and imagine that you are floating gently out of your body and moving to the site you have chosen. Begin to notice and describe the details of what you see.

3. When you have seen enough, float back into your physical body and take some deep breaths. Do some stretching and give yourself a few moments to come back into the room.

4. Write down everything you can recall from your experience. Bear in mind that you may feel as if you are just making things up, but when you do eventually visit your chosen location, you may be surprised to find that you are were more accurate than you thought you would be. Be willing to take a risk, even if it means being wrong.

CONNECTING WITH YOUR HIGHER AWARENESS

We all have a higher self or consciousness that helps to guide the course of our lives. The higher self is a part of our mind that acts as a bridge between the physical and spiritual realms. Getting in touch with your higher self can help you make positive life choices, and the process of psychic development will automatically strengthen your connection to your higher self.

The more attention you give to your higher self, the more likely you are to connect with it. Every time you listen to your intuition and act with integrity and honesty, you are enhancing your higher awareness. Getting in touch with your higher self may seem strange and awkward at first, but the more you practise it, the more you will be able to incorporate psychic abilities into your life. As you make contact with your higher self, you will feel more creative, calmer and in greater control of your life. This doesn't mean that you won't encounter problems; the difference is that you will able to handle your problems with greater creativity, confidence and resilience.

Meeting yourself

This exercise will help you to meet your inner guide.

1. Sit comfortably, breathe deeply, close your eyes and imagine that your higher self exists in a beautiful place of light and sound, and that the place is right above you.

2. As you breathe, visualize a bridge leading to your higher self and see yourself climbing onto it. As you enter your higher self you are surrounded by light, colour and sound. Take the time to explore.

3. When you are ready, see in front of you a full-length mirror. You realize that the image you see in the mirror is the real you, the ideal you – your higher self. To your amazement, your higher self steps out of the mirror and says, 'I am the most creative part of you. I see that which you do not. How can I help you?' The voice is kind, gentle and loving.

4. Sit down with your higher self and ask it what lies ahead for you in the coming week. Listen and remember what your higher self has to say. Your guide tells you that it is always with you, then melts into you so that you feel your true essence awakening.

5. Your heart is filled with hope. You are greater than you can imagine. As you leave, bring that feeling of inspiration with you to your daily life.

6. Walk back across the bridge and, as you do so, see yourself expressing your higher awareness in every waking moment.

7. Gradually open your eyes and make note of any insights that have come to you.

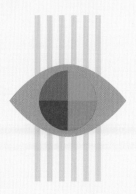

WORKING WITH CHAKRAS

You may already have come across the word chakra; it is a Sanskrit word that means 'wheel'. One of the easiest ways to understand the chakras is to think of them as individual radar terminals for the higher self.

There are seven major chakras in our body, each controlling different body systems and levels of the subconscious mind. They are the centres of energy activity in the body, handling all life energies for us; all energies experienced outside the body are picked up by one of these chakra centres and linked to the higher self. There the information is gathered and stored in your subconscious, and you can access that information through development of your psychic powers and by means of chakra-opening meditation exercises (see pages 168–9).

To tune into your third eye, allow yourself to become aware of the images that play in your mind.

Eyes wide shut

Information from your higher self can be received through all the chakras – and working with a chakra is a book in itself – but the forehead centre (or third eye, as it is also known) is most commonly associated with the development of psychic, and in particular clairvoyant, potential. The third eye is closely linked to the development of psychic talents, because it is associated with the pituitary gland, which is said to produce the chemical linked to visions and dreams; and with the pineal gland, which works as a light receptor. The pineal and pituitary glands must vibrate in unison for the third eye to be activated, and this can be achieved through meditation.

The third eye is always open, but can be drowned by the thoughts in your head. To become more aware of your third eye, you need to silence the chatter within your head. Sit silently, close your eyes and relax. Playing music without any singing can help this process. Become aware of images flowing in and out of your mind. Concentrate on the details and let the pictures remain for longer than just a flash, so that you can really take them in. Now you are aware of your third eye and, by making time just to watch the images play in your mind, you will develop a stronger awareness of it and will notice when you are picking up information from the subtle realms of thought, emotion or spirit.

THE SEVEN MAIN CHAKRAS

In India, the word 'prana' is used to refer to the energy that flows through the chakras. When you inhale, prana moves down the right side of the spine, and when you exhale it moves down the left side of the spine, creating a continuous current throughout the spinal column. The seven chakras are all positioned at major energy points along this pathway. Here is a brief summary of the chakras, the colours associated with them and the life aspects they represent.

- CROWN CHAKRA: Associated with the colour violet, this is located at the top of the head and represents destiny and divinity.
- FOREHEAD CHAKRA: Associated with the colour indigo, and also known as the third eye, this is located in the middle of the forehead and represents intuition and inner wisdom.
- THROAT CHAKRA: Associated with the colour blue, this is located in the throat and represents communication.
- HEART CHAKRA: Associated with the colour green, this is located at the heart and represents love and harmony.
- SOLAR-PLEXUS CHAKRA: Associated with the colour yellow, this is located in the solar plexus and represents personal emotions.
- SACRAL CHAKRA: Associated with the colour orange, this is located in the abdomen and represents creativity and healing.
- BASE CHAKRA: Associated with the colour red, this is located at the base of the spine and represents strength and survival.

Third-eye meditation

Your third eye is a doorway to your higher self and unknown potential. This meditation will help you open that doorway.

1. Relax your mind and body, and breathe deeply. Inhale slowly and deeply through your nose, holding your breath for as long as is comfortable, before letting it out through the mouth. Repeat for four more breaths.

2. Focus your mind on the space in front of your forehead and imagine a movie screen there. Don't try to think about what's on the screen; simply let images drift across it and focus on them as they come and go. Your third eye is opening.

3. Look for a colour on the movie screen and, when you see it, ask yourself what that colour could mean. Now look for shapes, and question yourself in the same way. As you do so, visualize yourself moving closer to the image until you can almost touch it. What do you see? What do you feel? Do you recognize it?

4. Now that your third eye is open, you can ask for a message. You need to be clear about what it is that you are asking for; you may want to write down a short sentence containing your question on a piece of paper.

5. Go through the process of relaxing and creating your movie screen. Watch the colours and shapes unfold and let the answer to your question reveal itself to you as words, images or colours on the screen. Just let the story unfold.

6. Record what you see. Does it make sense to you? Even if it doesn't make sense now, it might do so at some later date.

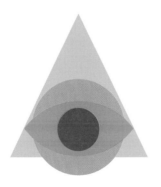

Facing fears

Your higher self responds only to positive energy. That is why throughout this book you have been encouraged to think, feel, sense and create positive energy in every aspect of your life. However, as you work to develop your sixth sense, you may find yourself having to face some of your hidden fears and negativity. Questions and doubts may creep into your mind. When this happens, call upon the brave warrior inside you; visualize yourself as the warrior of your life responding to events with courage and responsibility.

Wipe your slate clean

Use this exercise to build your self-confidence and trust in your higher self.

1. Imagine yourself standing before a large blackboard. Take the chalk and draw your problem or question.

2. Visualize yourself taking a step back from the blackboard and taking a seat as your higher self looks at the problem. Watch as the answer starts to appear on the board, wiping away your problem or question. Trust what you feel. Even if you don't actually see the answer in your mind, trust that the message has been sent by your higher self.

3. Thank your higher self, then imagine yourself leaving and feeling confident. Open your eyes and trust that the solution will present itself in your life.

4. Keep telling yourself in the days ahead that you are the wise one in your life, and that you have the understanding and confidence you need to face any challenge that life throws at you.

The art of living

When you are bold enough to listen to your intuition and follow your heart and your dreams, you will connect fully with your higher self. This is when the magic begins. Working with your sixth sense is an incredible journey that will last a lifetime, and many exciting experiences lie ahead of you, as well as challenges and frustrations. The true art of living – and of happiness – is found in how you react to the changing situations in which you find yourself. Let your psychic powers help you react with wonder, wisdom, optimism, courage, determination and, above all, hope.

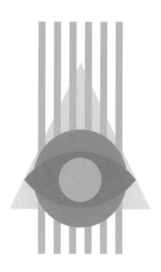

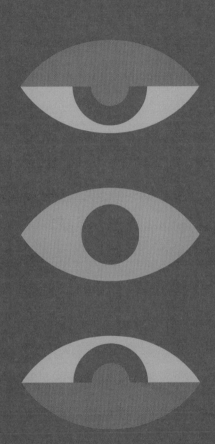

INDEX